RUINS

How God
brings hope
out of disaster

STEPHEN DERBYSHIRE

RIVER
PUBLISHING

God bless

Stephen Derbyshire

River Publishing & Media Ltd
Bradbourne Stables
East Malling
Kent
ME19 6DZ
United Kingdom

info@river-publishing.co.uk

ISBN 978-1-908393-60-9
Cover design by www.spiffingcovers.com
Printed in the United Kingdom

CONTENTS

THANKS

First and foremost, words can hardly express my thanks to my wife, Julia. You are, and have always been, a rock to me.

Thank you to the members of both City Gates and St Helens Elim. You allowed me to grow in my faith and make loads of mistakes on the journey to today. Thank you for your grace and for simply allowing me to be me.

Thanks to Jamie Coleman for proof reading the text.

Thanks also to Tim Pettingale of River Publishing for believing in this book and for his editorial advice and input along the way.

PROLOGUE

The first thought that went through my mind was, *"Please Lord, I pray no one is dead!"*

I was away at a conference with several staff members when a phone call interrupted our day with devastating news. Our partially completed new church building – over five storeys high – had collapsed. As shock and disbelief set in, I just wanted to know that no one had been hurt, or worse killed, in the sudden collapse.

There would be, I knew, at least 20 construction workers presently on site. But what had happened to them? At that moment it was unclear whether or not there were casualties. It seemed impossible that there wouldn't be.

I would find out the full story in due course, but for now I was confronted with the terrible truth that all we had worked so hard to achieve had been reduced to rubble. Our dreams literally lay in ruins. Where was God's purpose in all of this?

The building-in-progress was to be the new home of City Gates church, Ilford. I had worked in the town, serving the church, for almost 20 years. The church had long outgrown its building and this new centre was to be as much a spiritual sign for the area as a practical home for the church; a beacon of hope for the community. It was the culmination of a long journey, but also the beginning of a new chapter. The question was, how could we come back from such a big blow to our plans and still move forward?

I will seek to answer that question in this book, but first you need to understand a few things about me. Before the story of my involvement with City Gates could begin, God had to rescue me from the depths of a lifestyle that was as far away from Him as you can imagine. I was entrenched in drug addiction and consumed by a deep rage that would regularly surface.

To say that I took a very unconventional route to becoming a church pastor would be an understatement! But my story illustrates that God in His mercy is the Great Restorer. If God can take my life and do something with it, then He can help anyone. That is the message I hope comes across loud and clear in this book. Out of the ruins, God miraculously brings hope, and ultimately life.

1
ON THE TERRACES

Flashback to 1972 and you would find me on the football terraces. Violence was simmering, barely beneath the surface. One of my mates roared, "Get them!" at the top of his voice and I was well up for it.

Adrenalin surged through my veins as I ran, with hundreds of other Everton supporters, across the pitch towards a fight that had broken out on the other side. Out of the depths of my coat I pulled out my weapon of choice – a hammer. As I reached the tangle of bodies, I threw myself on top of them, swinging my hammer recklessly. I struck someone and immediately they crumpled to the ground. I grabbed someone else and head butted them. He slumped to the ground unconscious.

I could go on, but I want to spare readers the graphic violence of these days as much as possible. Suffice to say, my anger was boundless. On this occasion it was directed towards the hated Arsenal supporters, but it could have been anyone, anywhere. Football violence was merely a convenient outlet for the rage I felt inside.

At some point during the melee I felt a dull thud on the back of my head. Instinctively I ducked and then quickly spun around to see the red and white colours of the opposition. I lashed out and the man staggered backwards, arms flung out wide, narrowly avoiding my blow, then he scrambled away.

I pushed deeper into the crowd, hoping to injure as many people as I could. Then, in my peripheral vision I became aware of a raised hand holding a black object. I knew straight away that it was a gun and that it was pointing in my direction. I froze. Time stood still as I saw the muzzle flash. An eternity passed till the loud crack of the weapon discharging caught up with it. I managed to hurl myself to one side.

Around me the crowd parted as others became aware of the weapon and tried to avoid being hit. Another bolt of fire left the gun, another crack. I scrambled and dived over the heads of people around me. Someone behind me screamed, obviously hit. Seconds later the police arrived and swarmed all over us, hitting left and right with leather truncheons. Some of the Everton supporters managed to break through the cordon and fled back across the pitch to their stand in Gladys Street. I made sure I was with them.

I was clambering back over the barrier when I felt a hand on my shoulder. Whirling around, ready to retaliate, I heard a familiar voice.

"It's alright, Darby, keep your shirt on. It's me."

It was my mate, Trevor; his rat-like face dominated by his large nose.

"You're lucky, Trev. I thought it was the enemy. I was going to crack you one."

Trevor just laughed.

You would think that we couldn't get far enough away from the scene of such an horrific incident, but this was a routine Saturday afternoon for us. We settled back into our seats as though nothing unusual had happened. Then it dawned on us that we were one man short.

"Hey, where's Benny?"

We were briefly concerned that our friend had been hurt in the incident, but soon Benny appeared. He was grinning at us, sporting an impressive black eye.

Trevor waved him over and the short, stocky Benny scrambled over the barrier and sat down next to us. Now came the customary victory celebration and we proceeded to talk and laugh about how many of the opposition we'd "done".

Everton won two-nil that day, so all in all we were elated. On the walk back to the train station we looked out for any other stray Arsenal supporters that we could pick off – though we guessed that none of them would be stupid enough to walk away alone.

Just ahead of us we saw a small group of men burst out of a clothing shop, clutching garments in their hands. More fans running amok.

"C'mon," yelled Benny, "let's get some new gear!"

So we too dived into the shop. The shop assistants stood back, terrified, and just let us get on with it. I grabbed a pair of trousers and stuffed them under my coat. Trevor and Benny bundled up various items too. We exited the shop just as a group of policemen were piling out of two cars, but they weren't quick enough to apprehend us. Laughing, we ran down the road and disappeared down a maze of side streets.

"Luck day for us, eh Darby?" Trevor remarked.

"You're right. We just need to score some coke and we'll be flying high," I replied.

Benny roared with approval. His praise caused ripples of pride to run through me. This was what it was all about – running wild with your mates.

As we arrived at Lime Street Station we saw a family with young children running out of the station, obviously distressed. They couldn't get away fast enough. Pushing past them we saw a pitched battle taking place between Everton and Arsenal supporters and the police.

My adrenalin spiked once more and I had the urge to rush in. My hand reached inside my coat and felt the grip of my hammer. In front of us I saw a group of supporters descend on a nearby police car. They prized open the door and dragged the policeman out, then managed to roll the car over and set it on fire. Meanwhile, the sound of sirens filled the air and got louder and louder as hundreds of police reinforcements began to arrive at the scene.

I was torn between the desire to get involved and the voice of self-preservation. Common sense dictated a quick getaway rather than another fracas. Benny interrupted my thoughts.

"Let's get out of here," he called, pulling my arm. "There's always next week."

He was right. We skirted around the trouble as best we could and finally got onto a platform. We quickly boarded a train bound for St Helens and fell into some seats.

At St Helens we made our way straight to our local, the Sefton Arms. After downing three Black Velvets (a mixture of Guinness and cider), I began to calm down and feel a bit more like myself.

"I wonder if anyone's got any stuff," said Trevor, gazing around to see who was in the pub that day. He drifted off to have a nose around, but returned empty handed.

"Nothing doing boys," he said.

"Tell you what, let's have a scout around the town and see what's about," Benny suggested.

We drained our glasses, left the Sefton and began pub crawling across town. We must have visited another half dozen pubs, having a couple of drinks in each before, drunk and bleary eyed, we stumbled into a little pub jam-packed with people.

"Let's get out of here, we're not going to score," Trevor said.

"Oh c'mon," I said. "Let's see. If not, we'll head back to the Sefton."

Standing shoulder to shoulder in a corner, holding our pint glasses, we scanned the room and tried to see if anyone was handling any stuff. It looked impossible, but then a man appeared in front of us out of nowhere.

"I've got some good gear," he announced, having worked out that we were looking. He unzipped his jacket to reveal a plastic bag.

"What is it?" Benny wanted to know.

"Coke."

My heart leapt. It was what I'd been dying for all day.

"How much?" Trevor inquired.

"Eighty quid a gram," the main said.

"Hey, you're joking, right? Eighty a gram!" Trevor complained.

The guy shrugged. "Take it or leave it."

"Hang on a minute," I butted in. I wasn't about to let him walk away. I'd been longing for a buzz all day and here it was, right in front of me. I wasn't about to let Trevor screw this up by haggling over the price.

"Let's have a sample," I asked.

He opened the bag and brought out a small sachet. I dipped my finger into the white powder and dabbed it on my tongue. It tasted good. I washed it down with a mouthful of Black Velvet and told the others it was good stuff.

"OK," Benny put in, "we'll take half."

Minutes later all three of us were squeezed into a single cubicle in the Gents. Benny opened the bag and shook a line of the white powder onto the back of his hand. Trevor and I did the same. I took a deep snort. Like a rocket being launched, immediately my head exploded with sensation. I screwed up my eyes then opened them wide. The drunken stupor I'd been in vanished in an instant and in its place came a sharp, clear headed vitality. I could hear my heart pumping in my ears and I felt 10 feet tall. Between us we snorted the whole bag, there and then.

Outside the pub the cold February air bit into us, but our energy levels rose to a crescendo. I felt as if my body was trying to burst through my clothes. My skin felt taught and I was ready for action. We began to run through the streets, laughing and shouting like a pack of animals.

Shortly we arrived at another favourite haunt, the Plaza Club, and headed straight for the bar. I was talking ten to the dozen. I couldn't shut up. A few girls began to hang around us. Whereas normally I would be shy and hard pressed to say a few words, now I was full of bravado, talking, laughing, cracking jokes.

"What's your name?" I asked the girl standing closest to me.

"Janet."

"That's a lovely name," I told her, full of confidence.

"Really?"

Lying, I told her more of what she wanted to hear. Trevor and Benny had also sorted themselves out with friends and we all carried on drinking. We were able to score some pills at the club. I lost count of how many we took. The combination of coke and speed heightened my perceptions. I felt bullet proof, on top of the world.

As far as I was concerned, now was what my life was all about. Here. Now. This. I truly believed that it was me, and no one else, who was fully in control of my destiny. My family and friends, the mine in Haydock where I worked – all these things seemed a million miles away to me. The sound of Stevie Wonder's Superstition pumped out of the club's sound system and enveloped me. At that moment I felt like I had the strength of a hundred men.

Nothing and no one could get in my way. I was invincible.

This was what my lifestyle had become. I managed to hold down a job, so I had an income. Unlike some users, my supply of drugs wasn't about to dry up. I couldn't envisage a time when, like some poor helpless addict, I would be forced to beg, borrow and steal in order to meet the needs of my habit. Little did I know, fool that I was, what life held for me just around the corner.

I leaned back on the bar, full of arrogant swagger, my mind a swirl of disconnected thoughts, all white noise and not much sense. Benny nudged me out of self-reflection.

"Hey Darby, this girl reckons she's got some good stuff at her house. Shall we go?"

"What are we waiting for?" I replied. "Let's move it!"

Minutes later I was sitting in the back of a cab with my arm draped around the girl whose name I had already forgotten, eagerly anticipating a further cocktail of drugs. I knew that for the rest of the night, and probably half the next day, I would be completely wired. There would be no sleep for me until the effects wore off.

Trevor was crammed in next to me, a girl on his arm too.

"It was great meeting these girls, eh Derby?"

"Best thing ever Trev," I agreed. This, I decided, was the way I wanted to live the rest of my life: drugs and more drugs, a permanent escape from reality. I would leave my old life behind and journey on to who knew where.

2
GROWING PAINS

How was it that a pretty average kid growing up in St Helens turned into a reckless, violent, drug abuser? It's not a straightforward question to answer. There were a number of twists and turns in my story, and many contributing factors. All I can do is look back over my life and tell it how it was…

* * *

"No Mum, please!" I protested, tears streaking my cheeks.

"Don't be silly, Stephen, you'll have a great time. You'll see."

My mum tried to calm me down and make me see sense. I didn't believe her.

"I want to stay with you," I pleaded.

"Well you can't. You've got to go to school. Now come on!"

Mum pulled me by the arm, hustled me out of the house and minutes later half-carried me through the school gates in her determination to get me there.

The distant sight of the school had caused my stomach to churn. By the time we arrived at the building I was gripped by a powerful fear, and by the time I got to my classroom, it had completely overtaken me and I was hysterical.

My poor mum was exasperated, having to drag me right to my desk on a daily basis.

"Give over, please Stephen," she pleaded. "Nothing's going to happen to you here. Before you know it the day will be over and

I'll be back for you."

Her words didn't comfort me.

"I'll get you something nice in for tea," she tried.

But no amount of blackmail could win me over. I hated school and that was that. I didn't want to be there. At just five years old I was already experiencing deep pain. I can't really say where it came from. I guess I was chronically shy and didn't know how to deal with it. In the playground, most of the children in my class had managed to pair up or form small groups of friends amongst themselves. They played together as if they'd known each other for years. But I sat with my face jammed up against the school railings like the bars of a prison, wishing I would be magically transported back home to be with my mother.

Tears coursed freely down my cheeks and my whole world appeared black. Even the knowledge that my sister, Norma, was in the school next door to mine held no comfort for me. I felt like I was being punished. Each day at school was torture. It's hard to say why I felt so insecure, but I reacted to it unhelpfully. It was here that a wild, rebellious streak found its roots. I had been quite happy pottering around at home with Mum, but now she had abandoned me to Miss White, my class teacher for the next few years. Of course, every kid has to go to school and their mothers aren't abandoning them, but that's how my five year old mind perceived it.

Throughout school I became bored easily and it wasn't long before I began to attract attention to myself by becoming the class clown. I knew that it stemmed from my desire to break free from the confines of the classroom and be on the other side of those gates.

My relationship with Miss White did not go well. She was an unusual character and only had a single, rotten tooth in her head. For a while I thought it was a burnt chip! One day I felt obliged to point this out to her. The other children found this extremely funny, but naturally Miss White did not! I was made to stand in the corner of the room, facing the wall as punishment. However, far from feeling chastened, this gave me a great sense of achievement. Not only had I made the whole class laugh, I didn't have to do any work either.

From that day onwards life became a running battle between Miss White and me. I was constantly being sent to the headmaster's office where Mr Glover would give me a lecture and then make me sit outside to consider the error of my ways. I was more than happy to sit there, whiling away the time daydreaming. It felt like most of the time I was on my own, which actually suited me fine.

Eventually, due to my disruptive antics, I became well known throughout the school – and yet, I didn't have one person that I could actually call a friend. Even though I could act up and get people laughing, I found it incredibly difficult to strike up individual friendships. I found that certain people would just rub me up the wrong way and I would take a dislike to them – even hating them – for no reason. That's how I discovered fighting…

At the end of our road lived a family called the Tappers. They were a rough lot, including the girls. One day, as I was playing out in the street with some friends, one of the Tapper girls came over and hit me on the head with a toy gun. My head throbbed with pain and I began to bawl. I ran off towards our house.

"Mum, mum, she hit me!" I cried and the tears gushed.

"Who did?" my mum wanted to know.

Between sobs I relayed my sorry tale. The Tapper girl was a couple of years older and much taller than me. I was scared to go back out and play.

"Come here Stephen," Mum said, "I'll show you a thing or two."

I wondered what on earth she was up to. Why didn't she just put her arms around me and soothe the pain away? Instead she had me follow her out into the yard. She stood there with her fists clenched and raised in front of her, like a boxer, and made me copy her.

"Right son," she said, "the next time someone hits you, instead of coming to me crying your eyes out, this is what you do."

She proceeded to demonstrate to me how to hit someone effectively.

It wasn't long before I had the opportunity to try this out. James was a stocky little guy who hung around with me and my friends. One day he invited us to go around to his house to play in the garden. His mum was laying on snacks and drinks, so it was worth the trip.

However, during the course of the afternoon James thought it would be very funny to lock me in the garden shed. Outside I could hear the other kids laughing and playing, but I was frightened to death. For the next hour I had to bite my hand in order to stop myself from screaming out. I hated the claustrophobic, confined space. Sweat poured off me as paranoid thoughts invaded my mind about what or who I might be sharing the shed with in the darkness.

Finally, James unlocked the door and as a stream of daylight flooded in, I gingerly stepped out.

"Was you frightened Steve?" James laughed, his rather chubby face split in two by a massive grin.

I knew there and then that I would wipe that smile off his face. I lashed out and my fist hit him square in the mouth. As his expression changed from mirth to shock, I hit him a few more times. It made me feel a lot better.

In the midst of all the commotion his mother came rushing out into the garden.

"I saw what you did you little horror. What do you think you're doing hitting my James like that, eh?"

I looked at her with distaste and said nothing. Coming closer to confront me, she bent down and hissed at me,

"You're a nasty little piece of work and nothing good is ever going to come of you."

In the years that followed those words – and similar ones echoed by others – would continue to live with me. This day, however, I felt pretty good. Someone had crossed me and I had sorted them out – just like my mum told me.

My reputation as a fighter grew and it attracted other boys to me – usually to see if they could beat me. Then, when I was nine, I started smoking. It happened during the summer holidays. I was hanging around in Sherdley Park with a few other boys when one of them – Ricky Moore, a scruffy little kid with long hair and a big mouth – produced a packet of Woodbines from his pocket.

"Here, Darby, try one of these," he said.

I didn't really know what to do with the cigarette he thrust into my hand, but I didn't want to look soft either, so I put it between my lips and breathed in as Ricky held a match to it. I spluttered and choked, no doubt turning a shade of green. Ricky laughed.

"Darby, you're supposed to breathe it into your lungs, not swallow it. It's not food!"

From then on I decided I would get used to handling cigarettes.

Coming out of school one afternoon I lit up and started to walk home through the park. A group of boys from my class who had been needling me all day were in the park at the same time and they started to harass me. Inside I was boiling with rage, but I didn't want to let them see that, so at first I brushed it off and pretended I wasn't bothered. However, I knew a fight was imminent.

In a few seconds, the group of lads had surrounded me and one of them tried to punch me. I was too quick for him. I dodged out of the way and managed to give him a good kick, which of course was just the encouragement the others needed to attack. Despite being outnumbered I gave them as good as they gave me. I just went crazy. Lashing out in anger I punched, kicked, head butted and even bit my assailants.

As one of the lads went down I grabbed him by the hair. It had been raining a lot and there were some deep puddles around. I forced him face down into the nearest puddle and summoned all my strength to hold him there, ignoring the fact that his mates were raining down heavy blows on me. I wanted to drown him and I thought I had succeeded until I felt a pair of arms encircle me and haul me off my feet.

"Right you lads, I know who you are and I'll see you in the morning."

It was one of the teachers from my school.

"He started it, sir," said one of the boys pointing at me.

"I don't care. You're all for it. I want to see you all outside Mr Glover's office first thing in the morning. Got it?"

"Yes sir," they intoned.

I was speechless with rage and gasped to regain my breath. The fight was over, for now, but I glared at each face in turn and promised to avenge myself. Over the next few weeks I did just that, picking off those boys one by one and reminding them who was boss.

When I arrived home that day it didn't take a detective to work out what I'd been up to. My mum looked me up and down as I stood in the kitchen, surveying my torn, muddy clothes.

"Fighting again, Stephen? You only fight to defend yourself, remember, not to beat people up."

"But Mum," I protested, "I *was* defending myself."

"Well I don't believe you," she shot back. "Will you never learn?"

I didn't learn. For me, fighting was easier than talking. Talking required interaction with people and I wanted to avoid that. I expressed myself best by punching and kicking. My infamous reputation grew and grew.

* * *

Apart from this unpleasant side to my character, I had a reasonable childhood, especially considering that both my parents were strict Methodists. I did all the usual things that boys of that time did: I used to go train spotting and I loved going fishing with my father. I would sit with my fishing rod in my hand and think about nothing for hours on end. Just being surrounded by the peace and quiet of the countryside, with no one to bother me, was my idea of a great time.

I had a girlfriend called Lorraine who had lovely long red hair. We used to meet in the local park and sometimes I would hold her hand. Now and again we would give each other a peck on the cheek, which was exciting. Much more exciting than this, however, was when I got to go to a football match with Dad. My ambition in life then was to become a professional footballer and play for Manchester United. I also loved going to see rugby matches, especially to see The Saints, St Helens' home team.

Unlike other kids my age, we didn't have a television at home. Neither was I allowed to go to the cinema. I could never understand why.

"Dad, can we have a telly soon?"

"No, lad."

"But why, Dad?"

"Because we can't!"

We had many such conversations but Dad was never

forthcoming and I was none the wiser. I found it all very frustrating. Eventually, Dad did cave in and buy a TV, but I still wasn't allowed to go to the cinema. My parents told me that "the devil lives there." Looking back now, I can see that this was their interpretation of their faith, but it was years before I managed to pluck up the courage to go and see a film!

Sunday was the blackest day of my week. Sunday meant church and my parents forced me to wear my Sunday best – a shirt and tie, jacket and short trousers. Walking between my parents on the way to church I felt like a man condemned to walk the plank, approaching his doom. Mainly I dreaded the thought of any of my friends seeing me in this dreadful get up. As far as my peers were concerned, church was for wimps. I had to fight hard to keep my reputation in tact and stay on top of things.

The local Methodist church was as loathsome to me as school. I had to attend Sunday school and sitting amongst the children to sing in the kid's choir was a nightmare. I hated standing in front of the congregation and singing about Jesus. In truth, I didn't do any actual singing. I just looked at my feet, my hands shoved in my pockets and my mouth shut tight.

Every year the church took part in a "March of Witness". I guess it was meant to let everyone know that the church was alive and well in St Helens, but as far as I was concerned it was nothing more than a bunch of people walking the streets with banners and placards generally making fools of themselves.

I didn't understand what Christians were all about. They didn't seem to live in the real world.

Everything they did and said seemed alien to me and my parents were no different. Mum and Dad would say, "The Bible says this, the Bible says that" endlessly. Whenever I got into trouble I could anticipate the oft-repeated words:

"God sees everything, lad. You can't get away with doing wrong."

This had the desired effect of making me fear God, but not in a reverential way. I pictured God as some despotic monster, waiting for me to trip up so that He could beat me with a stick.

The church's youth leaders, Brian and Ruth Taylor, were the only people I felt I could talk to. They always listened to what I had to say and tried to give me helpful advice. But although they tried very hard to understand me – and I respected them for that – even they didn't know how to deal with me. I felt like I had no one to turn to and this caused me to retreat even further into myself. I put up barriers between myself and other people.

When I looked at the lives of the other kids who lived around my area, I could see that they lived a different life to mine. They didn't have to put up with all the restrictions I had to live with. I was an oddball. That was half the problem. I stood out, yet I wanted to belong. I wanted to be accepted, to fit in, to not be considered an oddity with strange beliefs.

Living in St Helens, with all due respect to the town, just added to my restlessness. Nine miles from Liverpool and twenty miles from Manchester, with a population at the time of around 250,000, it was the epitome of grey dullness to me, like living in a cemetery. There were grey buildings, grey streets and grey skies. It was abysmal. Row after row of terraced properties merged one into another from one end of the town to the other.

Unemployment was high and those who did have jobs received poor pay. Life held few surprises. Our family lived in a small district called Sutton. Not far from my house was Pilkington's glass manufacturing factory, which constantly belched out sulphurous fumes, the air always smelling of rotten eggs. Local residents suffered from chest ailments and poor health. Even people's curtains turned green!

It seemed to me that the people of my town were an apathetic bunch of lifeless individuals, which drove me to do anything to prevent myself from becoming like them. This led to further experimentation. My friend, Tom, lived above the Red Lion, one of the local pubs. One evening, Ricky, Mike and I were out riding our bikes when Tom asked if we wanted to come over and hang out in his cellar. We agreed immediately.

The cellar was dark and warm, and the smell of alcohol wafted up to me as I climbed down the steps. My parents, of course, didn't drink. Ever. In fact, I didn't know anyone in my social circle who did. The four of us sat around on some crates and chatted for a bit, then Tom asked me if I'd like something to drink.

"Lemonade," I replied, eliciting a slight snigger from my mates.

"Don't be daft, Steve," said Ricky. "We've got all this booze here! Ain't that right Tom?"

Tom looked a bit nervous, but he nodded his head and got up and began to look among the crates.

"What about this?" he asked with a grin.

It was a crate of Babycham, twenty-four bottles in all. We drank the lot. How I managed to get home that night is still a mystery to me. I was so ill the next day that Mum kept me off school. It took a few days for the effects to wear off, but I decided there and then that I liked alcohol. It was a new sensation. It made me feel grown up.

The focus of my week changed as a result. Weekends routinely involved some serious drinking, so Monday became a regular day for me to miss school while I recovered. But that was just the tip of the iceberg. I soon began to take days off whenever I couldn't face the thought of school. When I did turn up I sat at the back of the class, brooding and angry, wishing I was a million miles away from the place.

I looked around at my classmates and knew that we were poles apart. I would never fit in with them. They all seemed so eager and happy. I was the complete opposite. Looking back, I missed so much school that it's a wonder I learned to read and write at all.

When I was skiving off I usually ended up in a little café in Sutton, not far from where I lived. In the evenings it was frequented by a local gang of greasers called the Red Rose Rockers. Me and my friends, who also skipped school, would meet up there to hang out. We each took turns to be the lookout, in case the truant officer passed by. We spent our money on food, drink, fags and the café's pinball machine.

When we weren't in the café we were up to some or other mischief. One afternoon we visited St Anne's convent, which backed onto my house. The convent had extensive grounds which were very secluded and we had to scramble over a high wall to get in. We pinched apples off their trees and strolled around munching on them as if we owned the place. Suddenly we heard a yell. Looking round we saw a bunch of "penguins" (as we called the nuns in their habits) shouting at us to get out.

"Get lost!" we shouted back. So what if we were trespassing?

The angry nuns began to chase us and we beat a retreat, shouting abuse at them over our shoulders. Before we exited the place we saw a priest coming towards us riding a bicycle. He was either drunk or an extremely bad cyclist, as he was wobbling about all over the place. He took one look at us, exclaimed "It's you bunch of terrors again!" and then joined in the pursuit.

We ran all the faster, laughing and shouting as we went, and the priest tried to peddle faster to apprehend us. It had the effect of sending him more out of control than before, until finally he crashed straight into a tree. We were in hysterics. The whole episode must have looked like a scene out of a Keystone Cops movie – the drunk priest, flat on his back, and the nuns with skirts hoisted up, running after us full pelt. But they couldn't catch us and we scaled the wall and headed back down Monastery Road.

This road led to our den – a derelict, prefabricated house attached to St Anne's School. It was here that I learned to play cards for money. We also used the nearby off-licence to buy booze, convincing the shop keeper that the wine and cigarettes were for our parents. He sold them to us and never asked questions.

There was no electricity in the prefab, so we stole some candles from the church. This was how we came to be acquainted with the cycling priest. He'd almost caught us as we were absconding with his candles.

Sometimes a group of us would spend the whole school day at the den, especially during the winter. The local truancy officer managed to catch up with me a few times – which shocked and upset my parents, who were trying hard to teach me right from wrong – but this only made me more determined to do my own thing.

It seems that trouble always had a way of seeking me out. One warm afternoon, the second day that week I'd skipped school, I was standing outside the café smoking and messing around with my friends when a gang of lads from another part of town came sauntering down the road. Whispering among ourselves we planned an attack. By this time I always carried a weapon of some kind, for occasions such as these. I looked forward to a bit of trouble and embraced it when it came.

No words were spoken that day. We just eyeballed each other, rival gangs. Then, without warning, we broke into a charge. Fighting was a way for me to let out all of my pent up frustration. Standing back for a moment, I took out a catapult I had stashed in my coat and fired a stone into the group of lads. It hit one of our enemies in the face, catching him in the eye. His screams drew the attention of passers-by. I didn't stop to find out what damage I'd done, I ran like the wind. But someone had recognised me and reported me to the police.

Later that day the police arrived at our door to see my parents. They were devastated. As far as they knew I had been at school. The police cautioned me, warning me about my behaviour. They made sure I knew how much trouble I would be in if anything of the sort happened again. I was just relieved that the boy I'd hit hadn't been blinded.

My parents were very upset and saddened by my behaviour, especially Dad. He tried to reason with me, asking me why I did such things. I couldn't answer him.

Despite such brushes with the police, however, my behaviour didn't change one iota. I continued to skip school. I couldn't see any logical reason for going. Spending time with my friends seemed more beneficial.

One day my friends and I were sitting around in the den smoking and drinking. Outside the den we were surrounded by grassland and, out of sheer boredom, we decided to light a fire. We poured some lighter fuel on the grass and flung a lit match on it. It flared up instantly and very quickly went out of control. The wind wasn't particularly strong that day, yet it was still enough to carry the flames towards the occupied houses on the other side of the field.

We were amazed at how the dry grass caught alight and the flames leapt higher. The residents soon noticed the fire and people began running out of their houses. Someone phoned the fire brigade. We, of course, scattered. I looked back briefly to see that the fire had spread towards a block of garages near to the row of houses. Some of the garages, which no doubt had cars in them, were catching alight. We were going to do a vast amount of damage.

I fled the scene all the quicker after that. There was no way I wanted the police to pin this on me. After all, I had only been a spectator. I wasn't the one who'd struck the match that had started this.

For a little while after this incident I started attending school again. It was just too dangerous to go to the den. The police investigating the fire had discovered our hideout and were on the lookout for a gang of boys.

School hadn't changed. I didn't feel as though I had missed anything. The school was stuck in a time warp and didn't change from one day to the next. Feeling suffocated by the system, it didn't take me long to fall back into my old routine of bunking off. I started hanging around the café again and my friends and I took to roaming the town. It was normal for us to be found standing on street corners, swigging beer and generally being unpleasant, frightening people as they passed by.

One day, with Guy Fawkes night just a couple of days away, we bought some bangers. As we hung about we noticed a group of elderly ladies making their way towards us, dressed up to the nines. My friend whispered to me, "Let's give them a proper heart attack" so we lit a banger each and hurled them towards the ladies. Unfortunately, one landed on one of their heads.

"Help me! Help me! I'm on fire!" she screamed.

We ran off down the road, laughing at the panic and distress we'd caused. It was a typical, thoughtless display of trouble making. It's what we were good at.

During the summer our days were spent down at the local reservoir near the monastery. It was a large area flanked by lots of trees on one side and a major road on the other. We used to fish there and generally hang out, smoking, drinking and having a laugh. We had made a swing out of an old tyre and a long piece of rope, which was tied to the branch of a tree close to the water's edge. It meant that we could swing right out over the water, which was exhilarating, sometimes falling in then splashing back to shore.

One afternoon, some of my friends decided to go down to the reservoir after a very heavy downpour of rain. I declined to join them because I'd been drinking all morning and couldn't see straight. All I wanted to do that afternoon was lounge around at the café.

The reservoir was a deceptive body of water. Whilst the surface was quite still, strong currents ran underneath. Some of the boys were playing on the swing and one of them fell in. Almost instantly the current sucked him under and he was drowned. The first I heard of it was when some friends of mine rushed into the café and told me what had happened.

Sobering up instantly I ran down to the reservoir with them, arriving just in time to see paramedics retrieving the body from the water. The police had cordoned off the area, but from where I stood I could see that my mate's body had turned blue and bloated. His body was lifted onto a stretcher and taken away.

This awful scene lived with me for a while, but we were incorrigible. It wasn't long before the memory faded and my friends and I were back at the reservoir doing the same thing as before.

Most of the time my parents were completely unaware of what I was up to. Apart from the times when the truant officer, the school or police contacted them, they didn't know a thing. As long as I behaved myself in their presence, like the dutiful son that I wasn't, they were just fine. When I got into trouble, my mum just put it down to me being a mischievous boy.

My sister Norma wasn't interested in me and the feeling was

mutual. The only time we interacted was when we were arguing or fighting. When we fought, it was fierce. I recall one day a neighbour hammering on our door, wanting to know what was going on. She was convinced that one of us had killed the other!

My strict upbringing caused me to long for excitement and action. All the rules and regulations at home left me confused. There was never any explanation. I was supposed to know and abide by the rules and that was that. I just wanted to break out. I wanted to do incredible things that would cause people to recognise me in the street and want to be my friend. By the time I turned eleven I had a burning desire to explore the world. I just wanted to live life to the full.

Around this time I was friendly with a lad in my class called Paul. He was a bit arrogant and, even at his tender age, thought he knew all there was to know about living life in the fast lane! But although he got on my nerves at times, I still hung around with him. Our personalities were quite similar and he always had a bit of money on him.

One Friday afternoon he told me that his parents were going away for the weekend and his older brother was planning to have a party. Did I want to come? Of course I did. And to my amazement my parents let me go. Although I drank too much that night and was very ill because I had been mixing drinks, yet again the whole experience gave me a taste for the things that adults did and I craved them all the more.

The local café was patronised by all sorts of people. Consequently, as long as you didn't start a fight inside and you paid up front for what you ordered, the owners couldn't care less what people did. As a result, it was often the place to go for those who wanted to be able to take drugs in public without the threat of being caught by the police. I was a keen observer of the whole process. I would be playing on the pinball machine or sitting at a table, watching people exchanging little packages for money. I knew something was going on, but I wasn't sure exactly what.

I also noticed that a lot of people who smoked in the café were smoking cigarettes that didn't come out of packets. These were longer and a bit misshapen – fatter at one end than the other. Also, the smell they gave off was hypnotic. Sitting in this spicy, heady atmosphere, seeing people living a "freer" type of life created a strong desire in me to do the same. None of my friends were involved in drugs at that time, although we wanted to try them. We were friendly with a few of the adults who came into the café, and they were OK about most things, but they weren't about to share their drugs with school kids.

Eventually, I moved up to the Central Modern Comprehensive School, but within weeks I was bunking off classes there too. I continued to find it hard to build relationships with people I didn't know. It was too much effort. Instead I would spend lots of time on my own, occasionally hanging out with a few people I kept in touch with from junior school.

The only time anyone took any notice of me was when some of the older boys tried to bully me. I was a bit scared but determined not to show it. I retaliated with all my strength and they soon left me alone.

The only good thing about secondary school, as far as I was concerned, was that my parents gave me money for bus fares and dinner. Of course, I wouldn't spend it on those things. I would use it at the café.

The desire to try drugs was eating away at me. I couldn't see why I shouldn't at least sample one of those funny looking cigarettes. I just wanted one puff, to see what it was like. At the same time I was frightened about the effect that drugs might have on me, but I

31

wasn't about to show it. After all, I thought, what harm could I do to myself? Apart from their dreamy eyes, the people who smoked drugs at the café looked perfectly normal to me.

Eventually, emboldened by my desire, I approached a guy I knew at the café and asked outright if I could have a couple of puffs of his joint. He just laughed.

"I'm not wasting good stuff on a kid like you! One day, when you're older, you'll be able to have all the drugs you want."

3
FIRST EXPERIMENT

I shouted goodbye to Mum over my shoulder as I headed out the door, slamming it behind me. Freedom. I half-walked, half-ran up our road to the bus stop with a sense of anticipation. All week my best friends, John and Derek, had been going on about visiting St Patrick's Youth Club. It was a place where you could play pool, see if any "new talent" turned up (some girls found my brown curly hair attractive), and listen to soul music. Compared to our household it was like being transported to another world.

John and Derek were as reckless and wild as me, probably more so. They had both been suspended from school. Whilst bombed out of their heads on glue they had assaulted a teacher. I'd wished it had been me.

Walking through the doors of the church hall I felt on top of the world. Being with people my own age gave me a boost. Just talking, laughing and playing ball games with them made me feel like I was in the real world. I thought about the youth club I used to go to at Mum and Dad's Methodist church. Compared to this it was like a morgue.

I began a game of pool. I was just about to pot a colour when Derek called my name. I looked round and he was beckoning me to the back door.

"Darby, out here. Come out here."

"Give us a couple of minutes!" I called back.

"No, come now!" he insisted.

"Oh, all right."

I knew what was going on. It was common knowledge that a group of kids hung around in the alley at the back of the church to sniff glue. Although I drank and smoked, and wanted to try smoking weed, I wasn't attracted to glue sniffing. As I entered the alley, the potent smell of adhesive was overwhelming.

I stood next to Derek at the edge of the group and watched them hand around crisp packets containing the glue. Though I'd never been interested before, I now had the urge to join in and try it. Then Derek turned to me and said, "Why don't you try this? It's good stuff."

I wanted to belong; to be accepted; to feel a part of this group. I didn't want my friends to think I was a coward either, so I nodded. Derek took a crisp packet and poured some more glue into it. Then he took a deep breath and inhaled. Passing the bag to me he said, "That's how you do it."

I took the bag from him, stuck my nose into it and began taking deep breaths. By the time I had taken a few breaths, the sound of my breathing and the rustling crisp packet sounded amplified to extreme levels, as though a ton of steel pipes was clattering around in my head. I handed the bag to the person next to me and sat down, putting my head between my legs. My heart raced and I felt as though the alley walls were closing in on me. Dimly, I heard laughter and I imagined everyone was laughing at me. The night outside was black, but inside I felt blacker. I felt empty. Guilt washed over me.

My temporary dreamy state began to vanish and my mouth felt watery. My eyes began to smart. My stomach churned and threatened to erupt. I clenched my fists, determined to hold it down, but I had to vomit. My head was banging. I just wanted to go home.

As I sat on the bus home the guilt continued. I huddled in the back and refused to meet anyone's eye. I felt as though everyone could see straight through me and they all knew what I'd been doing. I felt dirty and used. I panicked at the thought of my parents confronting me about glue sniffing. I couldn't face that. Would they smell the glue on me? Would they tell by my eyes that I wasn't all there? Walking towards our house I wished I'd bought a packet of mints. I hesitated at the front door with my key in my hand and held my breath. I couldn't go in.

I turned around and hurried away in case my parents heard me. I walked slowly around the block several times, trying to drum up the courage to go in. Throughout my drinking escapades I had always gone home and my parents had never cottoned on, but somehow the glue sniffing had brought on an uneasy paranoia. I thought I would be found out.

Eventually I went home. Opening the front door I hurried through the front room, mumbling to my parents that I was tired and wanted to go straight to bed.

"OK love, see you in the morning," Mum replied.

Going up the stairs I marvelled at how easy it had been to deceive them.

The following morning I woke up feeling like death. My banging head persisted and my stomach felt like I'd had a good kicking. I got up and trudged into the kitchen. I couldn't face any food so I just drank a glass of water.

"Is that all you're having, Stephen," Mum asked, incredulous. "You're not feeling ill are you?"

"No, Mum, I'm alright," I replied, quickly turning away from her gaze.

"Well, make sure you have some lunch then," she said.

It was Saturday and that afternoon found me standing in the terraces at Goodison Park to watch Everton play. A cloud of depression hung over my head as I replayed the events of the night before. Before I knew it, the match was over and I had missed most of it. I was in a black hole of self-recrimination, unable to climb out.

After the weekend it was back to school and, as the week progressed, I gradually began to feel like my old self. By Thursday I was laughing and joking and my normally large appetite had returned.

When Friday evening came around it was like a replay of the previous week's events. Strangely, I didn't feel the same as I'd done the week before. I played some pool, secretly hoping that I would be called outside and offered some more glue. Sure enough, I was. This time the experience was different too: although I had the same dizziness and sickness, something was lacking. I didn't get the same high as before. But one thing was for sure: I had gone through a kind of initiation rite and I was now "one of the lads".

By Wednesday of the following week a new wave of excitement was rippling around the school. There was talk of a new drug. Just a couple of capsules could give you a massive, Nirvana-like high. It could save you from sniffing endless bags of glue or drinking loads of pints and, best of all, it was cheap.

I latched onto this immediately. The glue sniffing had awakened something in me. This was what I wanted – something that glue sniffing couldn't fulfil. Roll on Friday.

On Thursday evening I asked my mum if I could stay over Friday night with John and Derek.

"What for?"

"Everton are playing away and it'll be easier to leave with them early in the morning," I lied, hoping that Mum would swallow it.

"OK, make sure you take your pyjamas," she said.

I couldn't believe I was getting away with it. I smiled to myself; I'd done it. When Friday arrived I was hot with excitement. I took a bus into the town centre and met up with John and Derek outside the supermarket.

"Where are the pills?" I wanted to know straight away.

"Hold on," Derek said, fumbling around in his pocket. He pulled out a plastic bag, all the while looking over his shoulder, wary of being spotted by the police. In the bag were red capsules – barbiturates – known as Mandrax. They looked harmless enough.

"Have you got your Pound note?" he asked.

The three of us sat down on a bench and Derek opened a can of beer as I handed over the money. Then we each took turns to take the capsules, gulping them down with beer. After they were gone we decided to walk around the town centre for a bit, to give them time to take effect.

It wasn't long until John and Derek started laughing. One look at them told me that they were buzzing – grins plastered across their faces – but I was still sober. I wondered briefly if I was somehow immune to this particular drug, because nothing seemed to be happening to me. Then it hit me. A fog gradually swept over me and then caught me up in a euphoric cloud. I started laughing too. The slightest thing seemed incredibly funny. My brain was in a jumble and I couldn't think straight, see straight or walk straight. We tried talking to each other, but all we could do was utter absolute rubbish, which made us laugh all the more.

Our arrival at the youth club was the last thing I remembered. The rest of the evening was a blank. I was out of my head. Later, pangs of hunger began to gnaw at my stomach. I was ravenous. We headed to the local chip shop where I ordered a massive portion of fish and chips. The next port of call was the park. Although

John and I had planned to stay at Derek's place, we were in such a bad state that we couldn't make it there. The park was convenient. We stumbled around there, laughing and talking incoherently.

At around 2.00am we could see people coming out of nightclubs, drunk and noisy, calling for cabs and generally making a nuisance of themselves. We blended in well. But the hunger began to plague us again, so we finally dragged ourselves over to Derek's house. Arriving at his house we went straight to the kitchen and began making sandwiches – cheese, onion, pickles, tomatoes, gherkins and tomato sauce – all washed down with cups of tea.

Slowly we came back to earth and, as we did, we were overwhelmed with tiredness. I crashed out on Derek's parents' sofa, unable to make it upstairs. My eyelids suddenly felt like lead and my body a dead weight. Yet, sleep eluded me. I felt as though I was awake for most of the night. As soon as I drifted off, I woke up again. By morning I felt as though I had been punched in the head and my tongue was as dry as a bone.

Late morning, the three of us wandered back into the town centre and headed for the café. We discussed the previous night.

"We've got to do it again," Derek said.

"Yeah," I said. "Let's go for next Friday."

"You're keen Darby," John joked. "You've only just started."

I grinned.

"Now you know what you've been missing," said Derek.

I knew what he meant. Taking the Mandrax had made me feel free and uninhibited. It had a kind of bonding effect too. My friends felt as close as family to me. But then the guilt washed over me once again. *Family.* How was I going to face my mum? I reasoned that while I had gotten away with sniffing glue, surely she would notice there was something different about me now? I was no longer the old Stephen Derbyshire. I felt like a new person.

I eventually made my way home. I bought a newspaper en route in order to look up the football scores, so that I could keep up the pretence of having been to the match. I wanted to be able to speak about it accurately if questions were asked. When I opened the front door, Mum practically jumped off the sofa to greet me.

"You alright love?" she asked.

I froze.

"Look at your clothes! You look a right state."

It was only then that I realised how dishevelled I was looking.

"I, err, I got pushed about a bit on the terraces," I mumbled.

"Alright lad. Well, do you want your tea?"

"Yes Mum, I'm starving."

Mum cooked me some egg and chips while I had a bath and put on some clean clothes. Then I sat down and shovelled down the food.

"How did it go – the match, like?" Mum asked.

"Not bad. Two-nil," I replied.

"You were hungry lad."

"Starving."

I kept my head down, deliberately not allowing her to look directly into my face. I didn't want to give her the opportunity to notice anything "different" about me. Thankfully, she didn't.

* * *

During the months that followed, a great deal of my time was spent taking barbiturates and sniffing glue. This had the effect of unhinging me from reality. Rebellion grew like a force within me. I wanted to do whatever I wanted, whenever I liked. At school I was such a handful that my teachers were constantly reporting me to the Head, Mr Watts. Because of my bad attitude I received the cane on almost a weekly basis. Not that it deterred me – it just made me worse.

Mr Watts played his severe dictator role and I played my rebel without a cause role. We locked horns every time we encountered one another. "Trouble" was our common theme. Whenever trouble broke out at the school Mr Watts assumed that I must be the cause of it. He was usually right.

Along with my detachment from reality came a new sense of rebellious boldness where my parents were concerned. Whereas previously I had wanted to keep a low profile and pull the wool over their eyes, now I just didn't care. My bad attitude began to come to the fore at home just as at school. It didn't play well. My parents were exasperated by my lousy attitude and constant answering back, especially my dad.

"I'll clip you round the ear my lad," he threatened.

I shrugged this off. It didn't frighten me.

As is common with drug taking, I was now taking more barbiturates than before in order to achieve the same high as when I first took them. Instead of two capsules I needed six to get there. Getting the money to fund the pills got harder. I had to sell my bike, my fishing tackle, and a few other things to get the cash, and I was running out of things. My parents kept asking me where my bike had gone, and all the other stuff, but I was able to fob them off with lies. They bought my stories. The truth just wouldn't have occurred to them.

On Saturdays me and my friends would head to the "blow out" – a designated spot in the entrance of the large Co-Op superstore. I wanted to get stoned like some of the other lads around me, but I had no money. A few others were in the same position and so we discussed going shoplifting to steal some stuff to sell.

All the mischief I'd committed until now was child's play compared with theft. As we set off on our first attempt I was terrified. A couple of the lads went into a menswear store. My legs turned to water. What would happen if I got caught? My father would skin me alive.

I picked up three pairs of trousers and a couple of shirts and went into the changing room. I quickly put one set on over my own clothes and came out carrying two pairs of trousers and one shirt. I returned these to the rails and walked out of the shop holding my breath. When I was certain I'd gotten away with it I exhaled and experienced a different kind of high. I had stolen something and not been caught. This set the pattern for things to come.

At home, the rows with my parents increased and I began staying out for entire weekends, whether they liked it or not.

"I'm off Mum," I grunted.

"Where to, Stephen?"

"Just off, right? It's nothing to do with you."

I would stomp out the door, banging it shut behind me, oblivious to her feelings.

I tried to avoid Dad, but whenever he saw me, he tried to reason with me, to find out what was wrong.

"Stephen, what's happening to you?"

"Nothing. Nothing's wrong with me Dad."

I had no intention of getting into a question and answer session with him.

"You're changing, lad. You're not the same," he said.

I thought about this for a moment and I could sense the guilt welling up inside me. I had to push it down.

"Like I said, Dad, nothing's wrong, alright?"

After every such confrontation I would leave the house and quickly forget all about it. I had no interest in dialoguing with my parents. All I was interested in was what I could take that would transport me to another place. I wanted more out of life; something new.

The youth club no longer held any attraction for me and I had toyed with the idea of going to London. I'd heard that the drug scene was faster and wilder there than in Merseyside. That's how I found myself one evening in the back of a friend's car on the road to Wigan. Not London yet, but it was a start. These "friends" were older and more experienced in the life I was getting involved in.

We were on our way to Wigan Casino, which was used as a disco on evenings and weekends. It was a big step up from the youth club. The age limit was eighteen, which I wasn't, but the cashier didn't bat an eyelid as I handed over the admission fee. Inside the casino was huge, the darkness pierced only by the relentless strobe lighting. Upstairs was a large balcony with tables and easy chairs where we spent most of our time. Here we could take drugs freely and undisturbed.

My friends had given me some "French Blues" which combined amphetamine and barbiturate in one pill. Reckless as ever, I took ten of them. Along with these I was smoking. By now I had graduated to smoking dope – no longer the schoolboy dying for a puff or two. I was nearly a man, and accepted as such by my friends. I felt confident enough to take on the world and win.

Whilst under the influence, chatting up girls, which previously would have had my nerves jangling, was no problem. I would crack jokes, tell outlandish stories, and attract attention to myself by talking louder and faster.

The evening sped by and I discovered I'd lost all sense of time. I recalled entering the club at 9.00pm. It seemed like half an hour had passed. Now it was 2.00am. We all bundled back into the car and laughed and chatted our way back to St Helens.

My relationship with Derek and John was on the wane. These new friends of mine, Reg, Frank, Tolly and Sweep, to name a few, were all older, wiser and more experienced than I was. I aspired to their lifestyle.

In due course the car pulled up outside someone's house and we all trooped in. Whose house it was I had no idea. I didn't care. I was one of the boys – I belonged – that was all that mattered.

I felt very different the next morning, however. Where had all my confidence gone? All my inhibitions and fears returned like a slap in the face. My friends had warned me to expect this. It's what happens when you are coming down. Worse than this though was what was happening to my body. I was in unbelievable pain. It felt as though someone with a powerful grip had a hold of my intestines and was twisting them, trying to tear them out of my body. Gritting my teeth I put on a brave face, but I felt like death. As the hours wore on my head began to thump. It got louder and heavier. As before, I longed to go to sleep, but sleep wouldn't come.

Arriving home on Sunday afternoon, I stepped through the front door and all I could think about was my bed.

"That you Steve?" Mum called from the kitchen.

"Yes Mum," I replied wearily. "I'm going straight to bed. I've been up all night, I've got to sleep."

"OK love," Mum replied, resignation in her voice.

At last, sleep was sweet.

The Wigan Casino became my regular haunt. It was where all the action was: loud music, crowds, girls, and every kind of drug available on the market. Being part of that scene gradually became my normal way of life. Like a chameleon, I adapted myself to fit in with this new crowd of people. But I did so unwittingly, not realising the changes that were happening in my life. I was completely unaware of how my personality was changing. I thought I had never been more aware of myself or in touch with my mind and feelings. How wrong I was.

One particular Friday night I found that I couldn't get hold of speed for love nor money. Standing around with the lads, smoking dope, drinking and complaining about the lack of drugs, I caught sight of a few guys tripping on LSD. Previously I had never been interested in taking acid, but I was so bored and frustrated that night that I was willing to try anything.

A guy approached me. He must have taken one look at me and seen that I was interested. He held out his hand. Across his palm lay strips of cellophane. A closer look revealed microdot tablets, no bigger than a pinhead, navy blue in colour. I was mesmerised. I wanted to try one. The guy asked for a Pound for them. I duly handed over the money and took one straight away.

Like so many other times, at first nothing happened and I thought I had been cheated. But after about half an hour the drug kicked in. Suddenly my mind felt as though it was being separated from the rest of my body. I was floating. I was lost; totally outside of myself. Everything I turned my gaze onto looked bigger and better than it did in reality. The colours were more vivid and everything was vibrant. It was like I was watching a glossy movie and I was the star.

In due course, I left the party with my mate Reg. After being stoned, once again I was ravenous. We stopped by a local fish and chip shop and I put in a large order. I stuck a cigarette in my mouth but realised that I'd run out of matches. I asked the man behind the counter for a box and he threw one over. As I looked up, however, everything took on a surreal quality and reality became wildly distorted. The box of matches gliding towards me suddenly seemed to have grown in size to about 10ft and I thought it was going to crush me.

I cowered and staggered backwards, all in slow motion, my face a picture of horror, convinced I was going to be killed. I thudded into the window of the shop and stayed there, unable to move. I knew something was wrong with me, but I couldn't shake it off.

The man behind the counter looked at me in utter amazement. As the proportions of my world shimmered back to normal, I tried to laugh the incident off.

"Oh, thanks mate, I just slipped."

As Reg and I left the shop we began walking down the road, eating our chips, and once again my perception of reality rippled. I saw a bright red bus coming down the hill towards us. For a few moments I truly believed that I was bigger than the bus, and that one kick from me would catapult it back up the hill. The next thing I knew, I was going to do it. My legs had carried me into the middle of the road, right in the path of the bus. Reg stood on the pavement staring in disbelief for a moment.

"Hey! Darby! Come back!" he yelled.

The bus came relentlessly forward and I stood there immovable, determined to deal with it. Reg dropped his chips, darted over, grabbed my arm and hauled me back onto the pavement just in time.

"What're you doing Darby? You're gonna kill yourself!"

Suddenly I was snapped back into reality. I owed Reg one and I knew it. What on earth had possessed me?

The whole of that summer was a blur. I pursued a daily diet of drink, dope, speed and now acid as well. My life was one long trip.

Of course, all of this cost money, so I was shoplifting as much as I could, when I managed to coordinate mind and body to do it. As yet I hadn't been caught, but all that changed one night after school.

I was desperate for drugs that night so I went into the Co-Op intent on coming away with something. Walking up and down the aisles I thought about what I could sell quickly and decided on a pair of trousers.

In the changing room I slipped them on and put my own trousers on top. When I thought no one was looking, I casually headed for the door and tried to slide out. Just as I reached the exit a gruff voice spoke behind me.

"I have reason to believe you are stealing. Would you please come with me?"

I was paralysed with fear and the man already had his hand on my shoulder anyway. What would happen to me now? He dragged me off to a side room where I was told to sit down. I felt very sorry for myself. Shortly, some plain clothes police officers arrived to speak to me.

"Who are you working with?" one of them asked me.

At this point it dawned on me that they didn't know very much. They were just fishing around. Some of my old arrogance returned and I reclined in my seat. I looked up at them with a smirk on my face.

"Clever little boy, aren't you?" one of them said with contempt.

I shrugged, pretending not to care. They continued to question me, but I refused to cooperate.

"Come on, lad. Tell us who you're with."

I laughed.

All of a sudden one of them lunged forward and smacked me round the head with a wooden coat hanger. It nicked my skin and the cut bled profusely. I was stunned. These were the days before political correctness, when sometimes the police meted out justice on the spot!

"Right," the other officer said, "let's get you home."

When I arrived back home, flanked by two detectives, clutching my head, blood stains down one side, my mum became hysterical.

"What have you done to my son?" she shouted.

In the background my sister Norma began to cry.

Still holding my aching head, I sat and listened, hugely embarrassed, as the police explained to my mother that I had been caught shoplifting. Mum, however, was having none of it.

"Nonsense," she told them. "My son is no shoplifter."

The police could see that they were getting nowhere, so they quickly got me to make a statement then left. A couple of weeks later my mother lodged an official complaint, saying that I had been assaulted, but nothing ever came of it. Because of my treatment by the police, for a brief time my parents and I were allies instead of enemies – but this didn't last.

At secondary school I was ever more rebellious and it's fair to say that all the teachers hated me. The feeling was, of course, mutual. I was openly defiant. Most of the teachers didn't want me in the school and I certainly didn't want to be there. The younger kids all looked up to me as a rebel. I was their hero. My peers admired the way I stood up to the teachers and tried to copy my example.

The answer to my school misery came in the form of my music teacher, Miss Halliwell. She reminded me of a field mouse, little whiskers and all; her half moon glasses perched permanently on her nose, which twitched from time to time. She never walked anywhere, she scurried.

One night my mates and I were at the end of term summer dance which always finished off the year. We were stoned as usual. The dance was held in the school hall and at one point I sat down on the stool next to the piano. An idea came to me and I shared it with the boys.

"Hey, wouldn't it be a laugh if Miss Halliwell came to play the piano in Assembly tomorrow morning and it didn't work?"

"What do you mean Darby?" one asked.

"Look, I'll show you," I said.

I opened the lid of the piano and began detaching all the wires from the keys. Eventually the whole piano was "disconnected".

"You're bad you are, Darby," someone commented. "I can't wait to see her face!"

Neither could I. The next morning I sat at the back of the hall, watching and waiting with baited breath as Miss Halliwell scurried into the hall and seated herself at the piano. With a nod from the Head to begin, she lifted the lid and enthusiastically attacked the keys to bring in the first hymn.

Silence.

She tried again with a puzzled expression. Nothing. Sniggers rippled around the hall and soon the place erupted into all-out uproar. Miss Halliwell flapped around, flushed with embarrassment. My practical joke was an unqualified success. The Head was fuming and dismissed the school to their classes. It wasn't long until I was summoned to his office.

"Derbyshire," he began. "I understand that you are responsible for damaging the piano." He didn't even pause for me to offer some kind of excuse or defence – he had been waiting for years for an opportunity to dismiss me, and a golden one had fallen into his lap.

"Go home and get your parents," he ordered.

So I went. I had to tell my parents what I'd done. They accompanied me, tight-lipped, back to the school. We were ushered into Mr Watt's office and he got straight to the point.

"Mr and Mrs Derbyshire, we have decided to expel your son from this school. This incident has been reported to the police and no doubt you will be hearing from them."

My father did his best to try to reverse the decision, but Mr Watts wasn't about to let this one go. He was adamant. He wasn't going to put up with me any longer.

But while my parents despaired, I was elated. This was great – exactly what I'd wanted. Put out the flags – I was free!

As we exited his office, I overheard Mr Watts take Dad to one side and say, "Mr Derbyshire, I'm sorry to have to be saying this about a young lad, but I'm afraid your son will never be any good."

4
THE HARD STUFF

"I'll catch up with you later, Darby," Benny called to me.

"Yeah, see you later," I replied.

It was three in the afternoon on Friday and I had just stepped out of the cage that transported the miners up from the coal face. After being thrown out of school I had managed to get a job at the local pit. I was relieved that my shift was done and I could look forward to the weekend. Work didn't hinder my lifestyle – it was just a means to an end, to fund my habit. The night before I had been dropping acid and had drunk enough beer to sink a ship.

The effects had taken time to wear off. Working underground, rats occasionally ran over my boots as I chipped at the coal face, and today the lingering effects of acid had turned them into terrifying monsters with huge teeth. They leered at me, threateningly, and I barely stifled a scream.

"You alright, son?" one of the older guys asked.

"Yeah, yeah, I'm fine," I said and carried on working.

After being expelled I had made a few visits to the Unemployment Benefit Office and had been referred to the Youth Employment department. Here I was offered a place on a training scheme to become a deputy manager with the National Coal Board. I had exuded confidence at the interview, mainly due to the speed I'd taken earlier, and so breezed into the job. I was accepted for training and here I was, down the pit, learning the job.

The first week I received my wage packet I felt like I'd just backed a Grand National winner. Nine Pounds was a fortune to me then! It was a tremendous feeling having money that I had worked for myself. I decided to give my Mum two Pounds towards the housekeeping. She was delighted. Now that I was working, my parents relaxed a bit, safe in the knowledge that I was at least trying to do better than I had in school.

Dad took me to one side.

"Stephen, your mum and I have decided that because you're trying hard to do well at work, you're free to come and go as you please, as long as you let us know where you are and that," he said, beaming.

"Hey, that's great, Dad," I replied. "Yeah, I'll let you know what I'm up to," I said, knowing full well that I couldn't and *wouldn't* tell them a thing.

"Good, good," Dad said. "We're proud of you son, you're doing well."

Pangs of guilt pricked my conscience. Here I was stuffing myself with drugs and alcohol and my parents thought I was "doing well". But my guilt was short lived. I was soon out doing what was now a natural, even essential part of my life.

Most nights after work were spent down at my local, drinking with friends. It was nothing for me to drink four or five pints and then get a takeaway to soak it all up. My wages never stayed in my pocket for long. At the weekend, it was back to hanging out at the Wigan Casino, getting bombed out of my skull on as many drugs as I could swallow or smoke. A fascination for the opposite sex began to take hold and I was never without a girl, but the relationships I formed were shallow and meaningless.

All my dope smoking hadn't turned me into some kind of chilled out hippy, as you might expect. My love for fighting hadn't waned one bit. In fact, it had increased and I had got better at it, and grown stronger, as drugs fuelled me with both energy and fearlessness.

Wigan Casino was a popular gathering place for young people from all around that part of the world. Gangs from both Liverpool and Manchester would ride over in convoy on their scooters or motorbikes. Whether they were Mods, Rockers or Skinheads, hundreds of drug-taking youths would descend on the place, looking for a bit of trouble, and they always found it.

One Friday night my friends and I were propping up the bar there, steadily getting drunk, when some lads came up to us and told us that a group of our friends had been attacked by a vicious group of Scousers in Wigan town centre. They had beaten them up badly; some had broken ribs, while others were covered in cuts and bruises.

We downed our drinks and left the club, hurrying into the town centre, only to find ambulances taking away our wounded. There was no sign of the Scousers, but apparently their parting shot was that they'd be back at the Casino next week and they promised to finish off the rest of us.

When the following Friday came around we were prepared for war. We had taken some speed earlier than usual so that our heads would be reasonably clear and our confidence high. All week we had been discussing and planning what we would do.

"I've been trying to get hold of a shotgun for the last couple of days," Benny said, "but there's nothing about."

"A shotgun? What for?" I asked.

"To do their kneecaps in and then kill them," Benny replied without a hint of humour.

We all burst out laughing.

"Leave off, Benny," said Mike, who was built like a tank and thoroughly dangerous in a fight. "We don't need guns, just these." He held up his fists.

"I agree with Mike," put in Reg, who in my opinion only had half a brain and usually agreed with what anyone said.

I didn't say a word about what weapon I was going to use. I always carried a weapon and I'd been thinking for a while about tooling up with an axe. I went looking for one that week and found one in a hardware shop. It was a handy size and fit neatly into the inside pocket of the sheepskin coat I'd stolen from a Chelsea supporter at Lime Street Station, just after I'd beaten him up.

We had a plan of action. A lookout would be stationed out of sight in the car park of the club. As soon as the Scousers were sighted, the lookout would tip us off and we would charge out and "welcome" them. The plan worked, although the gang didn't turn up until 10.30pm, by which time we'd had a few. But this didn't hinder us. If anything it made us more aggressive.

"They're here! They're here!" someone shouted.

That was it. People streamed out of the club like a river, some of us to fight and plenty as spectators. Some people were knocked down and trampled in the chaos. Even the club doors were wrenched off their hinges. My heart was pounding.

As I rushed out into the cold night air all was confusion. At first I didn't know friend from foe. I came face to face with a guy on a scooter. He was wearing a green khaki jacket with writing all over it. I didn't really see his face. I just knew that he was one of the enemy and I was going to have him. I landed a blow that sent him sprawling on the ground. We fought and I was consumed with anger. "I hate you!" I yelled. Blows were punctuated with words. "That's for hitting my mate ... that's for coming down here ... that's for thinking you could beat me."

All around me the fight was intensifying. There were shouts

and screams, arms and legs flailing. I looked around for another opponent when an idea entered my head. I went over to a scooter lying on the ground, opened the petrol cap and let the fuel leak out. Then I took out a match, lit it, and threw it on the ground. Instantly the flames roared up and people nearby scattered. Within a very short time the fire spread. Standing back I surveyed my handiwork. This was the icing on the cake.

The sound of shrieking sirens filled the air and the crowd began to disperse. I blended into the moving tide of people. I could hear people asking who had started the fire. I smiled to myself that with one flick of a match I had ended it all.

Walking away, I ducked into the first pub I came to and headed for the toilets. I washed myself down and looked in the mirror.

"Steve, you were great," I said to myself – and I really meant it. "You've done a good job tonight."

* * *

My job, which I'd enjoyed at first, was beginning to drag me down. I only stuck it out because of the money, which went straight from my pay packet into the hands of drug dealers or barmen. I went through cash like water.

By the time my sixteenth birthday arrived I felt like an old man. I had packed so much into my life – drinking, partying, drug taking – that I felt old for my age. And yet, there was still something missing from my life and I knew it. I wanted something that would really bring a zest and freshness to it.

A number of my friends had by now graduated to using hard drugs. They were constantly urging me to try some, but I was hesitant. I thought that if I started taking "junk", as we called it, I could easily get out of my depth. There were horror stories about people who had overdosed on it. Then I had seen first hand the shocking state of some people's arms – where they had tried to inject themselves but had missed the vein, or the vein had collapsed or, more commonly, where the needles and syringes they'd used had been dirty.

I knew it could have an adverse effect on people and change them, physically. I had always been conscious of dressing well and I'd noticed that Benny, similarly fashion conscious, was beginning to look very scruffy and dirty. People on drugs seemed to go downhill fast.

On the other hand, because I wasn't doing the same stuff they were doing, I was losing some connection with my friends. That sense of camaraderie and belonging was fading. I was beginning to feel like a bit of an outsider and I didn't like that. I lived for the time I spent with my friends. To lose them would be the end of my world.

I knew that my days working at the mine were numbered. Getting up early every morning was such a drag, especially in the middle of winter. I wasn't fully awake until lunchtime, so my work got done only with huge effort.

One Wednesday evening I made my way down to the Sefton. I had enough money to buy a couple of drinks and obtain a small hit of a couple of pills. With a drink in my hand I sat down next to a guy named Dennis. He was a few years older than me and I respected him. Dennis seemed to know everything and be in full control of his life. I knew for a fact that he was on hard drugs, but he looked fine on it and talked sense. He held down a steady job and had a girlfriend. As I sat down to talk to him, I knew he had just hit himself up because his speech was slurred.

"Hey, Darby! How come you haven't cranked up yet?" He mimed injecting his arm.

"No way, Dennis. I don't fancy sticking needles in my arms."

"Darby, listen to me, listen to me," he drawled. "Take my

word for it. Nothing will happen to you. It just makes you feel good man."

I said nothing, but shook my head and took a sip of my pint. Looking at Dennis I could see he was having difficulty focusing his eyes and he had a soft, sleepy expression on his face. It had the opposite effect to speed, where everything comes into sharper focus and people's eyes get larger and brighter.

Throughout the evening Dennis kept on at me.

"Look, Darby, I've got a clean needle and syringe here. I'll even let you have some gear for free – no charge. Go on, don't be daft. Take it."

I was struck by the offer of free gear. No one who was serious about using drugs gave away anything for free. On the other hand, I had heard that a lot of people who were on drugs had been given their first shot for free. I reasoned with myself that if I missed this chance of taking drugs I would be out of my circle of friends forever. I was reminded of the first time I sniffed glue – a similar situation. "Drugs can't do much to me…" I told myself, "…as long as I control it." I looked around the table at my other mates, aware that they were all on it. They appeared to be as normal as ever.

Standing up I said to Dennis, "Come on, I'll give it a go."

"That's it, Darby," he smiled, patting me on the back. "I knew you'd do it, given a bit of time."

We ducked into the Gents and stood facing each other in the end cubicle. My nerves were frayed. I watched as he prepared the heroin for the syringe. A thought flashed across my mind: *what would my parents think?* But then they'd never known about any of the other things I'd done, so why should this be any different? Anyway, I was at the point of no return.

"Roll your sleeves up," Dennis instructed me.

Holding out my arm, Dennis wrapped his belt around my

upper arm and I balled up my fist as he tightened it. A vein in the crease of my arm bulged out.

"Don't worry, Darby, you'll be great in a minute."

He rubbed my arm and I looked away. I couldn't stand the sight of the needle going in. I felt a prick and flinched. Then I glanced down and watched as Dennis pushed the plunger down. He drew it back a little and some blood came out, then he pushed it back again.

Immediately, I saw an explosion before my eyes. I started to fall backwards, hitting the wall behind me and sliding down to the floor. My ears became blocked and my body felt as though it was wrapped in a gigantic cushion. My limbs turned to jelly. I had a funny taste of peppermint in my mouth and my lungs were heaving. For the next five minutes I felt like an alien lost in space. Nothing was familiar to me. Yet I was relaxed and unafraid. I tried to speak, but the words were difficult to form. In a funny kind of way I was very happy and comfortable. Minutes passed before I stood shakily, rolled my sleeves down and slipped my jacket back on.

"How do you feel?" Dennis asked.

"Fine. A bit shaky though," I replied.

"Don't worry, you'll soon get used to it," he grinned.

Walking back to our seats through the crowded pub, I told Dennis that it was a fabulous experience. He laughed.

"Told you, Darby. You didn't know what you were missing. Trust me, I'll never put you wrong. Oh, and by the way, the next one you have you'll have to pay for yourself."

I decided then that I wouldn't bother wasting any more money on pills, I would stick to heroin. It was pricey, but I was sure I could manage it on my wages.

For the rest of the evening I drifted in and out of consciousness.

One minute I was in the middle of a conversation with someone and the next I had nodded off. Then I'd wake up and carry on where I'd left off. It was odd. By the time the bell went for last orders the effects of the drugs had worn off.

Over the next couple of days all I could think about was getting my next hit of heroin. Back at the Sefton I scored once more, in the same cubicle as before. Dennis taught me how to inject myself. I wanted to learn as quickly as possible, so that I wouldn't become dependent on him. By the end of the first week I was using hard drugs successfully, shooting up for myself.

Of course, I began to develop a deep craving for the drug that was like nothing I had ever experienced before. It was constantly on my mind. *How will I get hold of some stuff? … Have I got a clean needle?*

When I couldn't get access to any heroin I plunged into a deep depression, punctuated with aggressive outbursts. My poor mum didn't know what to do with me.

"Steve, come and have some tea."

"NO! I'm not hungry!" I would shout. In fact, I was rapidly losing my appetite.

"There's no need to shout, love," Mum responded, clearly hurt.

"Just shut up, will you?" I responded callously. I just wanted to block out the fact that I was causing her pain. I couldn't face it.

* * *

Days and weeks passed. The weather changed and the evenings were getting lighter. Spring was on its way. I hardly noticed. Hours merged into days which merged into weeks and months. Time was lost on me. All I was interested in was having enough drugs for a fix. I was now cranking up on a daily basis. How I managed to carry on working I will never know, except that I was driven by the need for money. But the cash to feed my habit was getting increasingly tight. Soon my costs would overtake my income.

Inevitably, craving turned to desperation and I hit a new low. Desperate for money I turned to burglary to generate funds. A few friends and I teamed up – we all had the same needs. During the day, one of us would size up a warehouse or jeweller's store or a house, to see how much security they had and how easy it would be to break in. That night we would return to do the job and take what we wanted – things that could be sold easily for cash. We would divide up the proceeds among us.

The first few times I was terrified of getting caught, but my hunger for drugs provided the motivation for me to follow through. I knew that I would do whatever was necessary to get money. After a few jobs, however, I became fearless. I knew that the money from the robberies would stop me from worrying about keeping up my supply of drugs, so I was able to relax and enjoy myself again.

When it was my friend Mike's birthday, the lads decided to treat him to a night out in Blackpool at the Mecca Club. We hired a coach for the event because we knew that by the time we'd finished, no one would be in a fit state to drive anywhere. The night began well. On the motorway we had a party on the coach, cracking jokes and laughing, drinking and cranking up. There were a few girls with us and those of us who were on our own chatted up the single ones.

We eventually left the Mecca Club around 2.00am. The coach was parked nearby, next to another coach with some youths from Liverpool on board. As we approached they hung out the windows and shouted at us.

"Hey, you Woolybacks! D'yer wanna fight?"

We ignored them.

"Hey, Woolybacks! We could easily 'ave yer!"

Since I'd been on heroin I hadn't gotten into any fights, but with this taunting I could feel the old feelings of hatred rising up in me. We were filing back onto the coach when a brick came crashing through our coach window and hit one of the girls in the face.

That did it. We rushed off the coach and ran after the guys who had thrown the brick. We chased them through the car park. One of them tried to dodge between two cars, but I was too quick for him and managed to grab him by the hair and pull him to the ground. He struggled for all he was worth but I held on for dear life. There was no way he was getting away from me. He was a big guy, much taller than me. I knew if he managed to get to his feet I would be at a disadvantage.

Thus started a furious fight. I was completely blinded by rage and determined to beat him to death if necessary. I carried on until someone grabbed me from behind and restrained me.

"Darby! Come on now, you're gonna kill him."

I tried to push away whichever of my friends it was, but they wouldn't let me go. It wasn't until I heard sirens in the distance that I came back to my senses.

By the time we got back to the coach the police had arrived, blocking the entrance and exit to the car park and cornering us like rats. They made us all get off the coach and said they were taking us to the police station.

I was frightened, but I refused to show it. The reality of what I had done to that guy – the thought that I might actually have gone on to kill him – hit home. I didn't want to spend the rest of my life in prison.

At the police station we were all herded into a room and a few of us at a time were led out to take part in an identity parade. I was picked out. I wanted to be sick. I was thrown into a cell and, in due course, interviewed about the night's events. I refused to speak. I thought it was best to keep my mouth shut, in case I incriminated myself, or anyone else. In the event, it didn't matter because the police still charged me with grievous bodily harm and malicious wounding.

My father was called and he came to bail me out. He was very upset.

"You done it now, son," he said wearily. "You'll go down for this by all accounts. What on earth possessed you to beat up that lad like that? Are you mad? What's your mother going to say?"

I wasn't worried about my mum, I was worried about myself. I knew I wouldn't last a day inside – I'd go berserk with withdrawal. In fact, I needed to crank up right then and I didn't have any gear on me. I had to get hold of something soon.

* * *

When my court case came up the trial lasted several days. Eventually, however, the judge was forced to throw it out because there just wasn't sufficient evidence. It was a massive relief. That night we all celebrated wildly by cranking up and drinking into the early hours of the morning. Later, I heard that the guy I had beaten up had gone permanently deaf in one ear.

Not long after this incident I lost my job. I had failed to turn up to work too many times following big nights out. When I did turn up, I lacked concentration. After that I drifted through various jobs and the outcome was always the same: eventually I got fired.

Heroin had now taken over my life. I couldn't get enough of it and I hated the thought of not having enough money to buy it. Through all of this, my poor parents didn't have any inkling of my real lifestyle. I rarely saw them anyway. I was out constantly, either at the pub or partying somewhere.

Like so many addicts, my appearance started to go downhill. I had always made sure I looked the business when I went out, but now my appearance was of no consequence to me. I was much thinner, my complexion was pallid, and I had long, greasy hair hanging down my back. It was too much effort to have a wash and I would wear the same clothes for days on end.

I had also developed a dull ache in my side that wouldn't go away. I felt ill most of the time and I would often vomit for several days in a row, especially after a big drinking bout. I put all this down to the drugs, but the pain in my side persisted. Eventually, reluctantly, I was forced to go and see my GP who, after examining me, referred me to a specialist.

At the hospital I underwent intravenous pyelography and it revealed that I had nephritis – inflammation of the kidneys. The disease had advanced so rapidly, probably due to my drug abuse, that I was told that my kidney would have to be removed.

Amazingly, the news didn't have that much of an effect on me. All I was interested in was getting rid of the pain. However, after the subsequent operation, the pain was worse than before the kidney was removed. I drove the nurses mad by constantly bawling out in a loud voice that I was in pain. They gave me pethidine – a highly addictive analgesic – every two hours. In between the bouts of pain I lay in bed with a ridiculous smile on my face.

I was discharged after a couple of weeks and it didn't take me long to get back into the swing of things. As usual, money was short. It seemed pointless to me and my friends to keep breaking into shops and warehouses, and travelling miles to turn over a house wasted too much time. It seemed more sensible to go to the source. Pharmacists in small rural areas were easy to break into.

A friend of mine called Froddy had a transit van. We set off early one morning and within a couple of hours we were in a small village on the outskirts of Yorkshire. We spotted a small pharmacist's shop without any bars on the window and, best of all, no alarm. When the shop opened I went in and bought a packet of mints, sizing the place up at the same time. I spotted the controlled drug cupboard on a wall in the back room. When I came back out my friends looked at me expectantly.

"Well?"

"Easy as pie," I replied. "The staff are as thick as two short planks."

We all laughed.

That night we broke in and made our way into the back room. Locating the cupboard, we ripped it off the wall and carried away the whole thing. We made off with large quantities of barbiturates and amphetamines. We were jubilant. It had been so easy.

Thus continued our pattern. When I wasn't stoned I was driving round the country with my mates, robbing pharmacists, using the stuff we wanted and making money on the leftovers. I still managed to keep working during this time, doing menial jobs.

Finally, however, this activity led to a showdown with my parents. We had just done over another pharmacy and it was my turn to hide the sack of goods until we could get together and sort it out. I arrived back home and had the sack with me in the kitchen for a couple of minutes while I made myself a cup of tea. I thought everyone was out. I decided there and then to have a look through it and see what we'd got. As I was poking around I suddenly became aware that I wasn't alone. Mum was standing behind me.

"Steve, what have you got there love?" she asked. I could hear the fear in her voice. I didn't want to answer her, but her voice became a little louder.

"Steve?" she took a step towards me. "What have you got in that sack?"

I saw no point in lying any more, so I simply told her everything. I was a junkie and I had resorted to theft to service my habit. I was stealing to survive.

Mum lost it. She ran upstairs screaming for my father. Dad went mad and confronted me.

"How long have you been on this rubbish?" he demanded.

"Ages," I replied indifferently.

"What?" my mum cried. I thought she was going to pass out. "How come we didn't know?"

"You never asked me."

"Don't be cheeky, son," warned Dad. "Answer your mother."

I wasn't prepared to continue the conversation, so I got up and walked out of the house, carrying the sack over my shoulder. I went and stashed the stuff in a derelict house not too far away. By the time I returned home I knew my mum had told my sister Norma. Her tear-stained face told the story.

"Why, Steve?" she whispered. Her voice was hoarse from her crying. I just walked past her and went to bed.

The next morning as I made myself a cup of tea, my mum told me that she had been in touch with Mr Hesketh, my probation officer for the last couple of years. She had told him everything I'd disclosed to my parents the night before. I was really angry.

"What did you tell him for? He can't do anything for me!"

"How do you know that, Steve? You've got to get help from somewhere. He might be able to put us in touch with people who can." Mum sounded desperate.

I was fed up. Why couldn't they just leave me alone? I was getting on alright by myself, but now that they knew, they would be on my back every minute of every day. I wanted to leave home.

* * *

Mum arranged an appointment for me with Mr Hesketh, which

of course I didn't want to go to. But on the other hand, he held the power over my freedom. Reluctantly I went along to see him.

"Now, Stephen, what's all this I'm hearing?" he asked.

"It's all true," I said. "So what?" I was past caring.

"Come on, lad. Don't take that attitude with me. I want to help you, believe it or not."

"Yeah, I've heard that before," I responded coldly.

The truth was, Mr Hesketh was the only person I could talk to. Relenting, I agreed to let him try and help me.

Unfortunately, it came to nothing. Every door he tried was shut. At that time there were no clinics to help dry out drug addicts. Neither were there any counselling centres where one could get help. Hesketh drew a blank and I was left in the same position in which I'd started – looking to myself to supply my needs.

Leaving home was my next move. My parents had no idea how to handle the situation and being around them was becoming increasingly uncomfortable. Some of my friends were living in a flat not too far away and were prepared to take me in. The place was squalid, cold and rat and flea infested, but I didn't mind very much. The pluses outweighed the minuses. All the occupants were in the same position I was – all of them addicts.

Around this time the authorities were recognising that drug addiction was a growing problem, and that something had to be done before it reached epidemic proportions. At seventeen I was a registered addict. I had a prescription for Methadone from my GP, but it was totally inadequate for my needs. I had to supplement it with additional drugs.

I had a good friend called Stan who lived in the same block of flats and we would often hang out together, sharing our drugs. One night we had a wild party in his flat. There was always a party going on somewhere. The music we had pumping out faded into the background as we cranked up and got stoned. The next morning my first thought, as usual, was, "Have I got enough stuff to see me through the morning?" And this was followed by, "If not, where am I going to get some?"

Stan was asleep on the mattress next to me. I sat up, leaned over and shook him. I wanted to know how much stuff we'd got left. He didn't respond.

"Come on, Stan. Wake up! Have you got any stuff left?"

No answer. I was getting uptight now. My craving was kicking in.

"Hey, Stan. Wake up man."

Nothing.

Shaking his arm again I looked more closely at him. To my horror I saw that his lips were blue and I knew then that he was dead. I told the others what had happened and we knew we had to inform the police. Before we contacted them we cleared the flat of drugs and anything else that might incriminate us.

It wasn't long before the police arrived and an ambulance took Stan's body away. The police knew we were addicts and they didn't waste any time in questioning us. It was obvious that Stan had died as a result of drug-taking. He had choked to death on his own vomit.

Stan's sudden death was a terrible shock and had a profound effect on me. So much so that I resolved to give up drugs. That's when I realised that once you're addicted to drugs, it is incredibly hard to get off them without support. Six hours after deciding to "give up" the tremors of cold turkey hit me. I needed some drugs and I needed them now. From that moment on my habit increased all the more and I needed several injections a day to keep myself on an even keel.

Times were becoming harder but my cravings had intensified.

I didn't have time to drive out to the country to find a small pharmacy somewhere. I would have to make do with whatever I had around me. One day we broke into a pharmacy not far from the flat, but we got caught.

Once again I found myself in a police cell. Because of my insolent attitude one of the officers decided to have a crack at me. I head butted him and this was the green light for his comrades to lay into me. Half a dozen officers piled on me and gave me a good hiding. Standing before the Magistrate the next day I was black and blue from my encounter. Nobody seemed to care what state I was in. I was a criminal and criminals got what they deserved. I was remanded for a few weeks.

* * *

The hospital wing of Risley Remand Centre was abysmal. My fellow inmates included murderers and paedophiles – the scum of society – along with me. My first few days in "Grisly Risley" as it was known, were torture. I was going through major withdrawal and the medication I was being given to deal with it might as well have been aspirin.

I was locked in a cell by myself and had to slop out each day. I had reached the peak of my withdrawal and I was in agony. All I could do was scream out, tossing and turning on my bed to try and alleviate the pain. By the morning my bedclothes were wet through with sweat. My body ached all over. My bones felt as though someone had taken a hammer to them. Tangible hallucinations were driving me mad. I tore at my skin in an effort to rid myself of the insects that I imagined were crawling all over me.

I was paranoid and believed that the prison officers were conspiring to kill me. I was abusive to them and refused to eat any food in case they had poisoned it. Whenever they came into my cell

I would leap at them like a wild animal and try to bite them or tear their eyes out. Whatever I could do to harm them, I tried it.

They gave me injections of Methadone every four hours, which helped to calm me down for a short while, but then I would be in agony again. It took a long time for my pain to subside and for the fear and paranoia to leave me, but eventually I levelled out and gradually my thoughts became more rational.

After a few weeks of prison life I was actually the healthiest I had been in a long time. I spent a lot of time exercising in the gym and though the food left a lot to be desired, it added to my well being. Plus I was drug free for the first time in years.

My Dad often came to visit me. I sensed a change in him during those visits and when I asked him about it, he began telling me about Jesus. I didn't mind him visiting me until he opened his mouth and started talking about God. Soon, whenever he came it was all he wanted to talk about. But I had heard it all before. It hadn't had any effect on me then and it certainly wasn't gripping me now. I did notice, however, that the way my father was talking about God was different. He spoke as if he had personally "met" Jesus, the same way you'd say that you had met up with an old friend you'd not seen for a while.

"Son, no one can help you now – only Jesus. He most certainly can."

"Rubbish!" I said scornfully. "How can a man who died nearly 2,000 years ago help me? Once He was put on that cross, that was it for Him. Like it will be for you and me and the rest of us when our time is up."

"No, no, son. Don't say that. It's not true. You don't understand. Why don't you give Jesus a chance? Pray and ask Him to come into your life and help you. He'll answer you and do what you've asked."

All this talk irritated me intensely.

"Dad, if you've just come here to give me a sermon, I'm not interested."

Changing the subject I asked after Norma. After that he gave me news from home and let it drop.

After my remand, on the recommendation of my probation officer, Mr Hesketh, I was given a six-month prison sentence suspended for two years, followed by a further two years of probation. The judge ordered me to see Mr Hesketh once a week for the rest of my sentence. Right then if I had been instructed to kiss his feet I would have done it – I was getting out!

Coming down the steps of the court house I met up with my parents.

"Come home, Steve," my mum said. 'I'll make you a special meal tonight." She was overjoyed and relieved that I wasn't being sent to proper prison.

"OK Mum, I'll be home shortly," I told her. "I'm just off for a quick drink."

I had no intention of going home. My parents didn't see me again for another three weeks. Instead I headed straight for the flat. What did I do when I got there? I cranked up immediately and blew myself into oblivion. At this point in my life, if someone had offered me a million pounds to give up drugs I would have turned them down. Before long I had re-registered as an addict and my appearance regressed to its former shocking state.

I kept up my weekly visits to Mr Hesketh who began to despair of me.

"Look, Steve, you can't carry on living like this."

"Why not?"

"Because if you don't cut back your habit – in fact, unless you give it up altogether – you'll be dead before you're thirty.

The terrible thing was, I knew it was true.

5
A NEW LOW

"Are you getting up Darby?"

"What time is it?" I answered groggily.

"Three o'clock. Time to get up."

I dragged my tired body out of bed. I had slept in my clothes – again. The afternoon of any day was my morning. I looked out of the window, but struggled to focus. The brilliance of the afternoon sun and the birds singing outside washed over me unnoticed. I needed a fix.

I stood in the kitchen and ate "breakfast" – some Weetabix and a Mars bar. I tried to think about how I would be able score in order to see me through the next couple of hours. Irritability gnawed at my brain and I wanted to get moving as quickly as I could.

Gradually, the events of the previous night began to come back to me. I smiled to myself. I had been cranking up in the "shooting gallery" – an area of our flat designated for this purpose – with my mates. I must have had about six hits. After that I lost count.

I had been using Diconal, a new drug on the scene. The end result was very similar to heroin, but it was a lot cheaper and easier to score. It was an opiate-based drug and the rush from it was incredible. All night long me and my friends had sat crushing up tablets, dissolving them in water, then using a cigarette filter to draw off the pink solution. We would inject the remaining chalk.

Now my head pounded with heaviness and my arms were

aching and sore. I was a seasoned addict by now and I looked the part. I had abscesses on my arms where I'd had difficulty injecting, but had still managed to find a vein to use. When they got too bad I would use the veins in my foot.

I heard a knock at the door, but I couldn't be bothered to answer it.

"Hey, Darby, it's your dad," someone called.

A wave of embarrassment washed over me, which quickly turned to anger. How dare Dad come and see me here! As far as I was concerned, the fact that I'd said to my parents I was coming home, but as yet hadn't turned up, should have told them that I didn't want to see them. I knew that my father believed in God, but I thought he often behaved like Him too – interfering in my life as he pleased. Well today would be the last time he'd poke his nose in my affairs, I told myself. I would show him.

Coming to the front door I dispensed with any niceties.

"Why are you here? What do you want?"

"I'm here because you're my son," Dad said. "Your Mum and me are worried about you. You promised you'd come home weeks ago. You didn't, so I thought the next best thing was to come and see you."

I felt so angry that Dad had stepped into my world uninvited, that his words were lost on me. My hands automatically balled up into fists and my heart thumped. I was ready to explode.

I'm not sure whether Dad spoke any more words. My own seemed stuck in my throat. I was blinded by rage. My contempt for him and all that he stood for came pouring out of my mouth like a torrent. Hard, painful words. I pointed my finger at him.

"I don't want to see you or Mum ever again. Do you hear me? Forget you ever had a son, because I've already forgotten I had a mum and dad. Right, now clear off."

Tears streamed down Dad's face. The awful hurt I was causing him was so clear to see in his eyes, but I still didn't care. He turned and, with faltering steps, retreated, his head hanging down. Watching him go I slammed the flat door as hard as I could, rattling the building. I really wanted him to hear the bang of the door, as if to signal the finality of our last meeting; leaving him in no doubt about the barrier between us.

Returning to finish the breakfast I'd started, I callously laughed off the incident with my friends.

"Darby, you're really hard you are," someone commented. "Your old man really copped it from you."

Sad to say, I was actually pretty pleased with myself. I felt good. After all, this was exactly the image I wanted to portray to my friends – that I ran my life, my way. I looked out for myself. I didn't need my parents, or anyone else for that matter, breathing down my neck and checking up on me.

By early evening I'd had my fix and was sitting in front of the TV. Images flashed in front of my eyes, but I wasn't taking too much notice. Uneasy thoughts plagued my mind. So many questions that I didn't have any answers to. Why had I hit out at my dad? What was the point of it?

I wondered if I was going mad. I kept replaying the incident over and over in my mind. Out of pure concern for me, my father had come to see if I was alright. I had treated him as if he was my enemy.

I glanced over to my friends who were smoking dope and chatting. I couldn't talk to them about the way I was feeling; they would think I'd gone soft. I had to maintain the tough guy image. How else could I survive and still be with them? I tried desperately to push the guilty thoughts away. I couldn't cope with them.

* * *

Most nights I would be at the Sefton, drinking and having what I thought was a good time. Lately, some friends of mine had been telling me about a guy who kept coming into the pub – name of Pip Wilson, some kind of religious nut – who was driving them mad talking about God. I certainly had no desire to meet him. Living with my parents meant I'd had enough of God to last me a lifetime.

One Saturday night I was in the pub with my mates, standing at the bar waiting to order. One of my friends leaned across to me and motioned across the room.

"Darby, there's that religious freak, Pip. Shall I call him over?"

"Don't be mad," I said. "I don't want him anywhere near me. What he needs is some of this." I patted the pocket containing my drugs. "He'll know all about God then."

We got our drinks and went and sat in our usual spot. Pip glanced over towards us and immediately my friend raised his hand in acknowledgement.

"Hey, Pip! Come over here!"

Turning to me he whispered, "Let's have a laugh. We can wind him up."

I agreed, it was a good idea. Pip came over, not suspecting that we were going to have some fun with him. He was a short, nondescript kind of guy with glasses.

"Hello lads, how are you doing?" he asked.

"Fine, Pip," we chorused like a class of primary school children.

"That's good to hear."

He sat down at our table and began to chat with Tom, who knew him best. Tom later told us that before Pip had become a Christian he'd been well known for being a hard man. Some of the guys knew him because he had a reputation. Pip was now in charge of the YMCA in St Helens.

We tried to get him to talk about God, just so that we could shoot him down, but somehow he knew we were only trying to have an argument with him, and he kept steering the conversation away from that subject. He had quite a sharp sense of humour. He told some funny jokes which had us chuckling with laughter, yet they weren't dirty jokes. I wondered how he managed that. I decided that Pip was an OK guy – the first "religious" person I'd ever met who appeared to be relatively normal.

It was around this time that I wanted a break from all the familiar faces around me and I thought a holiday might be the answer. My main problem was that I didn't have any money, so my options were very limited. The next best thing would be to try and get a job working away somewhere. I'd had many jobs in between my illegal activities, but I was never able to hold one down for long.

When I landed a job as a waiter in a holiday camp – solving my going-away-for-free problem – I thought I would be there at least for the summer. The camp was in Prestatyn, north Wales. In the end, I was there for just three weeks, because during my time there I managed to stir everyone up about their low pay and encouraged them to take strike action. They did and I got the sack!

Frank was one of the caretakers at the camp. We got along well and hung out together. When I was shooting up, he would be smoking dope. We used to head to a local night club together to relieve the stress of the job.

One particular night, Frank and I were living it up, dancing with a couple of local girls when I felt my stomach muscles contract like I wanted to throw up.

"Frank, I've got to go to the loo," I said, doubling up and clutching my stomach.

"What's wrong, Darby" he asked.

I couldn't answer him, but he followed me into the toilet. Suddenly my energy levels had plummeted. I barely made it into the toilets. After I had emptied the contents of my stomach down the loo, I sunk to the floor and breathlessly told Frank,

"Listen, you've got to get me home. I feel like death."

I didn't sleep that night. I spent most of my time going back and forth to the toilet. I noticed that my urine was a murky brown colour. Something serious was wrong, but what? "I must go and see a doctor" I told myself.

But I didn't get myself to the surgery and the next day the pain and sickness had subsided, so I went to work as usual. The strike was scheduled for that day. It went ahead and was successful. We all walked out and the management agreed to give everyone a pay rise. We all went back to work and I was jubilant. But the day after our victory I was called into the manager's office and dismissed.

I headed home. I was somewhat relieved because I hadn't particularly enjoyed the job anyway. Travelling back to St Helens my mind was in turmoil. I hadn't seen my parents since the incident with Dad. I had, however, spoken to him on the phone and told him that I was coming home for a visit. He sounded pleased to hear from me and happy that I was coming home. I was full of guilt. I was only visiting for selfish, practical reasons, because I felt ill. I wasn't planning on staying.

Arriving home, I walked through the front door and my mum took one look at me and said,

"Stephen, what's wrong with you? You're all yellow."

I could hardly speak, I felt so terrible.

Mum made an appointment for me to see our GP, Mr Manning. When I got there, he glanced me up and down and began asking questions about my lifestyle. He asked where I was getting my syringes from. When I told him I got them from the local hospital's trash he was horrified.

"Stephen, you certainly have jaundice and I think you may have hepatitis. I'll arrange for you to have a blood test and we'll go from there."

I did indeed have hepatitis.

At the local hospital I asked the doctor what could be done.

"There must be some tablets you can give me," I said.

"No, Mr Derbyshire," he told me. "All you can do is have lots of rest, drink plenty of fluids and stop using drugs. And the most important thing of all," he said, handing me a piece of paper, "is to stick to this fat-free diet and you'll survive."

I spent most of my recuperation at my parents' house. It was stifling, but I kept reminding myself that it was only until I got myself back on my feet again, then I'd be off.

One thing that struck me while I was at home was how tranquil the house was. It was actually restful to be there. To my great surprise, my parents hardly ever badgered me about God or anything connected to Him. I felt that maybe they had finally accepted me and the way that I chose to live my life.

Most of the time I didn't see Dad, but I knew what he was up to. When he wasn't working he spent most of his time in his bedroom, praying and reading his Bible. "That's the best place for him," I thought. "Let him talk to God instead of me and we'll all be happy."

Mum had told me that they were now attending a new church. It was a Pentecostal one that was, apparently, lively and really friendly. I'd responded, "Good for you." But it did appear to be good for them. They both seemed happy and contented and there was no warring between the three of us.

After a while my strength returned and I made plans to move

out. My parents were sad to see me go, but amazingly this time they didn't make a fuss about it.

Away from my parents' house, I soon fell back into my old pattern of living. It was as though I'd never been away. Pip Wilson still came into the Sefton from time to time, and one evening while he was talking to us, he beckoned to his friend to come over and join us. I looked up as the guy approached our table and was shocked to see my friend Frank from the holiday camp in north Wales.

"Frank! What are you doing round here?"

"Darby! How are you? I see you're no longer yellow." He was just as surprised to see me. We laughed. It was nice to see a friendly face.

"So what are you doing here, Frank?"

"I've come to see Pip."

I looked at Pip then back at Frank.

"You two know each other then?"

Pip spoke up.

"Yeah, we're taking a meeting together at St Peter's Church."

St Peter's was in Parr, a parish not far from the pub.

"What do you mean 'taking a meeting together'?" I asked. I was confused. I was trying to work out what Pip and Frank could possibly have in common. Nothing, as far as I could see. But Frank, very clearly explained why.

"I'm going to St Peter's to tell people how I became a Christian."

Frank divulged this information at just the wrong time. I was taking a sip of beer. I nearly choked on it.

"You're what?"

"I said I'm going…"

"I know what you said, I just can't believe you said it. Have you gone mad?"

Both Pip and Frank began to laugh.

"I've never been saner in my life," Frank assured me.

I looked at the other guys sat around me. I didn't hold back. I told them how I'd come to know Frank and about the things we used to get up to. They were as surprised as I was.

"You're freaking me out Frank," I said. "You're suddenly a Bible basher? I can't believe it."

Pip looked at his watch.

"We'll have to love you and leave you fellas. It was nice seeing you all again."

He got up. My head was reeling. What was going on with Frank? Then Frank leaned over and said to me, "Darby, why don't you come along?" All the guys around me burst out laughing. I laughed too.

"Leave off, Frank. You go and have a good old singsong."

"I'll do more than that," he replied. "I'll pray for you."

After this incident, Pip's name kept cropping up time after time. He had taken some of my friends into the YMCA and provided food and shelter for them. He seemed to be a genuine guy. He was concerned about the way in which we lived our lives, without preaching to, or condemning us.

Pip had started something called the Fishnet Club, which was open on Sunday nights. Pip was the DJ. He played contemporary gospel music and throughout the evening would explain what each song was about.

The "club" was really just a large room within the YMCA. Pip had made an effort to turn it into a funky venue, with murals on the wall and coloured light bulbs that gave it a subdued vibe. Most of the people who went there seemed to me to be boring, with no sense of adventure.

My friends and I ended up there one night because it ran on

a Sunday, usually a dull night. With nowhere to go, the Fishnet was convenient and cheap. When we pitched up there we had already been drinking and shooting up so that we could relax and enjoy ourselves by taking the micky out of the people around us. It passed the time.

Amongst our group, Richie and Sweep were the biggest jokers. One night they asked Pip if they could liven things up a bit. They pulled out their harmonicas and began to play. The rest of us quickly jumped on the bandwagon and began to fool around. We hijacked the microphone and began to shout and swear, becoming totally uncontrollable. The other people in the club looked terrified.

Pip tried his best to calm us down but we wouldn't listen to him. In the end he threw us out and told us not to come back unless we could behave ourselves. We told him, in no uncertain terms, where he and his club could go.

After that I still continued to see Pip around the town, and we might stop for a chat, but whenever I got the sense that he was preaching to me, I just switched off. I would cut him off, making some excuse, and leave him standing there.

Things around me were beginning to change. Friends and other people I knew were beginning to suffer as a result of their drug habits. I knew people who'd had to have arms or legs amputated because of multiple abscesses that wouldn't heal. My friend Dennis – the guy who introduced me to heroin – had recently died of an overdose. I was faced with the fact that the life I was leading would soon be cut short if I didn't get myself together.

It slowly dawned on me in the cold light of day that I wasn't living at all. I was merely existing. There was a great big world out there waiting to be explored, and here I was – a habitual drug user – my life being run by the cravings of my body, like a wild animal caught in a trap, unable to set myself free.

I dreamt of freedom. In my fantasies I pictured myself climbing snow-capped mountains and surveying the vast expanse of landscape all around. Or I would be mixing with people from other cultures, eating different foods, experiencing exotic climates. Sometimes I would imagine that I had achieved a good profession, maybe working in a managerial position in a thriving company, or running my own business, earning lots of money. My imagination didn't stretch as far as being married and having children, but I guess I thought that was something that might happen in the distant future.

Seeing what was happening to my friends was a wake up call and it made me want to change, but that wasn't going to be easy. I kept trying to kick the habit, but within a few hours I started to experience cold turkey and the pain and the fear were too much. That meant I was soon back to robbing places, seeking out pushers, and then injecting, smoking and drinking.

One night it all became too much for me. I was buried in a thick fog of depression and it just wouldn't lift. It wound itself around me tighter and tighter until I could hardly breathe. I felt crushed under the weight of my desperation. I sat on my bed and surveyed the squalor of my surroundings, knowing that it wasn't in my power to escape. In my desperation I shouted out:

"God, if you're real, help me!"

There was no answer. I still felt the same.

"God, help me!" I shouted even louder, in case He hadn't heard me the first time. Nothing. A feeling of complete hopelessness washed over me. I was completely and utterly alone. I felt drained of all emotion. I knew that life definitely had more for me, but I just couldn't work out how to get out of this mess.

"There's only one way," I thought. I had been fortunate that day and had managed to make a bit of money. I went out onto the street and scored a large amount of heroin. I didn't tell a soul what I planned to do. I went back up to my flat where I knew some of my friends were shooting up. I said a few words to them and went into my room.

I mixed the drugs with water and contemplated my last few moments on earth. I was torn between fear and hopeless desperation. I wished that someone might come in and stop me, but no one did. My heart thumped wildly and I began to sweat. I really wanted help, but who could help me? I was on my own.

Help me. Help me. It was the sound of my own voice in my head. Hot tears trickled down my cheeks. "How did I get to this stage?" I thought to myself.

Memories of when I had first started using drugs and how they made me feel came crashing back. Those were such carefree days. I had so much courage; nothing could frighten me. I was out to impress my friends and have a good time – that was it. But now look at me. What a state I was in.

The need to end this downward spiral overwhelmed me. This was it, the last act of self-control, I was going for good. I would have liked somehow to say goodbye to my family, but I hoped that one day they'd understand. They would be OK, I reasoned. At least they had God.

Once the mixture was in the syringe I tied my belt around my arm, plunged the needle into a vein, and pushed the barrel up as quick as I could. The rush came powerfully, like an out of control bushfire surging through my body. I threw my head back and screamed. I couldn't breathe. I was suffocating, as though a powerful pair of arms were pinning me to the bed. I began to lose consciousness. I was fading away. I was gone.

* * *

Opening my eyes I was blinded by a brilliant white light. Was I in heaven? I couldn't understand how that could be, I wasn't a Christian. Jesus knew that, I was certain. So how had I managed it?

Then I became aware of people around me rushing around in a commotion. I tried to look at them but their faces were blurred and distorted. I could hear an incessant thumping sound. I tried to snap my brain into focus. Where was I? Maybe this was the reception area of hell.

Much later I drowsily gained consciousness. As I looked around me, I gradually understood that I was in hospital. Then I remembered what I had tried to do. I had failed to end my life. I couldn't do anything right.

My head felt like lead. My stomach was in chronic pain and my chest felt like it had been given a good hammering in a fight. Eventually, the ward doctor came to see me and told me what had happened. My flatmates had heard me screaming, but when they came into my room I was unconscious. My lips had turned blue and one of them had tried to give me the kiss of life while another called an ambulance. My heart had stopped beating in the ambulance and the paramedics had resuscitated me and put me on a heart monitor. It stopped beating again as I arrived at hospital and the A&E staff had got it going again with a defibrillator. Now I had been admitted to the recovery ward – alive.

"You're a very lucky man Mr Derbyshire," the doctor said, his voice full of contempt. "You've escaped death – *this time*."

Little did he know that I was as disappointed as he was. I had really wanted to die and here he was telling me I was lucky. If I'd had the strength I would have jumped up and punched him in the mouth.

Within a few days I had discharged myself from hospital. They were glad to see the back of me. I headed straight out onto the street and began hustling money for drugs. I went to live back at the flat and I carried on shooting up whenever I could. Life, if you could call it that, was exactly the same.

My one aim in life became self-destruction. Surviving my suicide attempt seemed to me the worse thing that could have happened to me. I now resigned myself to the fact that the drugs and I were lifetime partners until they finally claimed my life. All my waking hours were spent either using drugs or trying to get hold of the money for them. I wondered when it would all end.

My physical appearance hit an all time low. I wore the same clothes for weeks on end without washing them. I had scabs all over my body and my weight plummeted to under 8 stone. I was a pitiful sight, skin and bone, but I didn't care. My mood was permanently melancholic. Depression clung to me like a second skin. I no longer dreamed about what my life could be. To me it was utterly bleak.

The flat where I was now living was part of a large old house and all of the nine flats were occupied by junkies. There was no getting away from it. I was tied to them and they to me. Mum and Dad's house wasn't very far away and sometimes I had to pass it on the way home. At night I could see Dad's bedroom light on and I sensed he was keeping up a prayer vigil for me. Obviously it wasn't working. I was still very much the same, if not worse.

I was certain that my body couldn't continue to take the abuse I was subjecting it to and it was about this time that I began to search for other spiritual answers to the mess I was in. August bank holiday weekend was coming up and my friends and I decided to go to Lincoln Pop Festival. While we were there we noticed some people handing out leaflets. Stopping a young guy, I asked him what it was all about. He told me he was a disciple for the Children of God and that they were at this festival to reclaim "lost souls".

I decided to go to one of their meetings. They were different from my parents, mostly young people who seemed a happy bunch, singing and talking about Jesus. I sensed a real feeling of love there. I was told that the only way that I could be a successful Christian and get into heaven was their way – there was no other route. I perhaps would have joined them if it wasn't for that. My parents came to mind and I knew, deep down, that they were real Christians. They didn't belong to this group, so these Children of God had to be wrong and my parents right.

Back at home, some of my friends, who were also searching for meaning, were attending Spiritualist meetings. This seemed a lot more interesting to me. Some of the other guys had begun to dabble in witchcraft too and told me that there was definitely something in it. I decided to check this out, so a group of us went to Billinge, a small village outside town. It was after midnight when we approached a field where we could see the flames of a huge fire. Around fifty or sixty people were crowded around it, chanting and swaying with glazed expressions. Judging by the state of some of them, I was certain they'd been shooting up too.

The fire was roaring fiercely. When a strong wind blew over us, stirring up the fire, the people responded ecstatically, waving their arms in the air and chanting all the more loudly. A frenzy of excitement broke out. Then, as quickly as the wind had come, it stopped.

"Let's go home now," I said nervously to my friends, but they didn't want to go. The looks on their faces convinced me that they had been strangely caught up in the goings on. "Leave them to it," I thought. "I'm getting out of here." I turned and set out for home, walking the five miles back. I kept looking over my shoulder every few minutes and had an eerie sense that I was being watched. I felt very relieved as I finally put the key in the door of my flat.

My quest for spiritual meaning soon waned. Now, every time I injected I hated myself. I couldn't believe that no one on planet earth could help me. I felt shipwrecked; stranded on an island of my own making. I was so lonely. But for all my inner turmoil I never once let my friends know what was going on inside. At all costs, I reasoned, I had to keep up my tough image.

The despair I felt drove me at times to do things that were out of character even for me. Like knocking on the door of the local vicarage and telling the vicar that I was a junkie and needed his help. Sadly, I found no help there.

"Go to social services in town. I'm sure they will be able to meet your needs."

Door shut.

"So much for Christianity," I thought.

A new batch of heroin had come into town and we were all invited to a party where it would be circulated. After a good drink at a local pub, we went to the party. It wasn't long before we were shooting up. We passed around needles and syringes which must have been reused thirty or forty times. We had no qualms about sharing. When they got badly clogged up they were dumped on the floor. Within a few hours, everyone at the party was stoned. Suddenly, someone stood up and began waving a wooden crucifix in the air.

"Listen. You see this?" he said. He shook the crucifix, then pointed at himself and looked back at the crucifix. "I crucified this guy," he said. Then he sat back down. People thought this was funny and exploded with laughter, but his words hit me. For some unknown reason I sensed that, actually, what he was saying was absolutely true. I stood up.

"That's it, guys. I'm off now," I said.

"What's the hurry, Darby? Stay."

"No, I must go," I said. I began to stagger out of the room.

"You'll miss all the fun," someone said.

I didn't bother to reply. Getting home was uppermost in my mind. I ignored everyone and got out of the building. Outside it was difficult getting my bearings. I felt as if I was walking through treacle trying to get home. I was bouncing off walls and trees.

Eventually I arrived at a front door that was familiar, but it wasn't my flat. I realised it was my parents' house. I still had my door key so I fumbled about and tried to get it into the lock. My father must have been woken up by all the noise I was making because he came and opened the door. I staggered into the house and fell straight into the mainly glass door of the living room, crashing straight through it and landing flat on my face.

Dad knelt down beside me, stroking my head and asking me if I was OK. It wasn't a very sensible question, but as I was completely out of my head it seemed reasonable enough at the time. I grunted in response.

"Jesus is your only answer, Stephen," Dad said. "Why don't you just try Him?"

Couldn't he let up for once?

"Stephen? Stephen, can you hear me?"

I was really struggling to keep hold of reality.

Months later Dad told me why he was so insistent that I accept Jesus into my life. A few months earlier both my parents had been shopping in Liverpool. Dad felt a strong urge to pray, there and then. Mum and he stood in the middle of the shopping mall, debating what to do when Dad had the idea of going into the Anglican cathedral. Mum let him go off while she finished her shopping.

The cathedral had a prayer chapel down in its crypt. Dad made his way down there and, kneeling down, he felt God's presence very close to him. As he knelt, silently praying, he sensed that he was not alone in the chapel – someone else was standing by him. Dad kept his eyes closed the whole time during this holy moment and the man spoke. He began telling Dad all about his life and that the experience he and his family were going through would soon be over; everything would turn out alright. The words had the ring of truth and Dad believed what he was saying. He opened his eyes and turned around to thank the man, only to discover that he was all alone in the room. The person had disappeared.

This was another promise Dad had been given to add to a number of others God had already given him concerning me – that I would pull through and be alright; that I would become a Christian and serve God. But looking at me and the state I was in, it was incomprehensible that I could ever change.

That same night I lay helplessly on the floor and Mum and Dad carried me upstairs together. They lay me on the bed and Mum, who was a nurse, put me in the recovery position. They stayed with me all night, praying and watching over me. I was unaware of my surroundings. I hardly realised that I was still alive.

I awoke the next morning with a heavy head and a feeling of unreality. Here I was, lying on my own bed with absolutely no recollection of how I'd got here. Hours of my life were missing. As I crawled out of bed, the first thing I did was to pull a packet out of my pocket, assemble the bits together and crank up. Now I was ready to face the day and I made my way downstairs. Dad had gone to work, so it was just Mum at home.

"You up love?" she called from the kitchen.

"Yes, Mum."

"Like some breakfast?"

She looked serene and expectant, as though I should have

changed or I should be saying something to her. But I was still the same old me, as far as I was aware.

"Do you remember last night, love?" she asked.

I shook my head. I could hardly remember getting up and coming down the stairs, let alone last night. I had a light breakfast then took off, back to the flat. I just felt more comfortable there than I did at home.

Unbeknown to me, the reason my Mum was looking at me in such a strange way was because the night before, as they were both praying for me, I had responded to a question Dad had asked me.

"Son, why don't you give your whole life over to Jesus?"

"Dad, I want to, but I don't know how."

"Just say the words, lad. Just say the words."

So I did.

"Jesus, save me."

6
DISPELLING THE DARKNESS

"I wish I was dead."

Those words churned over and over in my mind, every minute of every day, every day of the week. So many friends of mine were here one minute, gone the next – all dead; all drug related. I longed for release from the problems that neither I nor anyone else could solve. Death alone seemed to be the answer. I actually envied my friends who had passed away. They were free now – no more hustling for money to buy drugs; no more excruciating cravings that reduced you to feeling like a wild animal. I wanted to be in that free-floating nether world, wherever it was, where I could be in peace.

But here I was, having to face the truth in the real world. Every single bone in my body ached. I felt like an old man. The pattern of my life was monotonous. Most of my days were spent sitting in a chair watching TV, after I'd had my morning dose of drugs. Images flickered before my eyes, but it was hard for any information to penetrate my drug-induced stupor.

By midday I would crank up again, maybe having something to eat, but only a Mars bar or something sweet, then I would sink back into the armchair. By the evening I would become more active because I needed to get out and get some money to buy drugs to see me through the next day.

During the day my energy levels were rock bottom. It took all the strength I could summon just to get up and go to the toilet. I wore the same shirt, trousers and socks day after day and slept in them at night. I never washed. My teeth were coated with a thick layer of plaque, so my breath was awful. Even my face was now covered with scabs, which I picked at if they itched, making them bleed. My hair was matted, thick with grease. My condition was extremely bad. I knew it and my flatmates knew it. The flat was like a degenerate human zoo and we were its inmates.

The veins in my arms had completely broken down and finding one to inject into was a problem, but this didn't deter me. I injected into my legs and feet, which made them very sore as the veins in that area of the body are unsuitable for taking in the chalk and residue. My veins blocked up regularly, which meant I developed abscesses all over my legs. I continued to pump heroin, and anything else I could get my hands on, into my war torn body. Not because I wanted to, but because I had to.

Depression was a constant companion. Even though I lived with others, I was very much on my own. I hardly spoke to anyone. I couldn't begin to express the way I was feeling. One of my biggest problems was pride. I had created a monster – a reputation that I was a hard man, uncaring, impervious to pain. For me to confess that this was a complete façade and a lie was a big step down that I wasn't prepared to take. I would torture myself with the thought that if my friends ever found out who I really was underneath my tough exterior, they would completely reject me. I couldn't risk that, so I kept it all to myself and lived in self-imposed exile from the rest of the human race.

I was still obliged to see my probation officer, to whom I was able to confide a few of my inner thoughts. Mr Hesketh genuinely wanted to help me and suggested that I see a psychiatrist. I did, but the experience was a waste of time. The psychiatrist spoke to me as though I were a slab of concrete rather than a person. He didn't understand where I was coming from and wasn't interested in me personally at all. He focused entirely on my symptoms, how they compared to the textbook and, therefore, how they should be treated. At this point in time I was one of a very small group of registered drug addicts, so dealing with people in my situation was new territory for the health service. They didn't quite know what to do with me.

I was in such a bad way that during one of my sessions with Mr Hesketh I broke down and cried. The pain and deep emotions inside me welled up and flooded out, deep convulsions shaking my body. I knew Hesketh felt overwhelmingly sorry for me, but he was utterly helpless. He put his arms around me and tried to reassure me that he would do everything in his power to help me to come off drugs and change my ways.

Instead of lifting my spirits and giving me hope, however, his words plunged me deeper into the bottomless pit. I knew, with every fibre of my being, that Mr Hesketh was powerless to release me from this living hell.

My feelings of degradation grew stronger each time I scored. Whenever I exchanged my money for that little packet, which I knew would do me no good, I experienced a debilitating cocktail of emotions from shame to sadness, to an all-consuming anger that could easily have led to murder.

Taking drugs was a nightmare. As I mixed the powder, drew it into the syringe and stuck it in my body, I hated the fact that I was so dependent on it. It seemed as though every time I cranked up the initial rush was the same as ever, but the effects would wear off faster, quickly turning into feeling ill and vomiting. Heroin had become harder to purchase, but I still needed my daily quota in addition to the methadone I was receiving. Whatever else I could get my hands on – barbiturates, amphetamines, even acid – all got crushed up and injected.

After years of taking drugs my body seemed to be rejecting them and yet craving them at the same time. I wanted to get away from it all, but how?

A couple of my flatmates and I talked about getting away to have a holiday. Within a short space of time I found myself accompanying them to Amsterdam – the nucleus of vice in Europe at the time. We shacked up in a seedy hotel that wasn't dissimilar from our flat back home. Then we headed straight for the red light district which wasn't far away. It was the only place we could think of where we might be able to score some dope.

We were right. No matter what country you're in, one pusher looks the same as another. I spotted a guy loitering inside the doorway of a night club. It was all done through eye contact. We eyed each other up and down and we both knew who we were – pusher and junkie. But I couldn't speak a word of Dutch and he didn't appear to speak English. Consequently I was ripped off. Going deep into the nightclub to crank up, it transpired that what I'd probably bought was talcum powder. Cold turkey was gripping me by now, so I started to drink a lot. Before long, though, another pusher turned up and I was able to score some more reasonable stuff which brought me back to normality.

I had planned to stay away from drugs in Amsterdam, but here I was. My body always let me down, forcing me to gravitate towards the urban underworld in search of drugs. However, the time away did do me a little good. My eating pattern was more regular and returning home I looked a bit healthier than when I'd boarded the ferry on the way out.

But as with so many times before, once I was home I was back on the treadmill of drug abuse as if I'd never left it. My motivation to live had been stirred by my trip to Amsterdam though. I realised that while I continued to live in this flat in St Helens, nothing was ever going to change. I had to leave. Once again my mind turned to exotic locations, particularly Morocco. The hot, humid climate, the easy going lifestyle, the markets and the food all appealed to me. I'd heard from friends who had been there that one puff of the local hash could transport you to the moon. I knew it was the place for me, but there was just one problem: I had no money. If I was going to go anywhere, never mind Morocco, I was going to have to get a job.

I didn't stop to think about whether or not I had any qualifications or whether I could actually cope with the rigours of a regular job, I just decided to go and get whatever I could. Turning over the pages of the local paper, I saw an advert for a role at the Rainhill Psychiatric Hospital in Merseyside. They wanted someone to train to be a psychiatric nurse. They also stated that the applicant would be expected to work as an assistant nurse before commencing their training. I decided to fill in the application form.

"I must be crazy," I thought. "There is no way I'm going to get the job."

My confidence was boosted when I sailed through the subsequent interview. I had borrowed some clothes and cleaned myself up. How I managed to be bright and chirpy on the day, I'll never know, but I was full of energy. Then the rug was pulled from under me – I was told I would have to have a medical.

"That's it," I thought. "Game over. I'm never going to get through that."

It was so depressing. There was always some obstacle that prevented me from getting on in life. By this time I looked a lot better than I had done in a long time. The sores on my legs and feet had healed up, but the track marks on my arms were still very much visible.

When the medical came around I wore a long sleeved shirt, having already made an effort to conceal the track marks using cover up make-up. I was nervous as I waited to go in. I felt like running away. In the event, I needn't have worried. When the medical officer took my blood pressure, I noticed that his hands were shaking. As I took a deep breath I got a nostril full of alcohol fumes. He was a drunk. A few days later I received a letter to say that I'd got the job.

* * *

I had been eagerly looking forward to starting the job, but during my first few days there I felt like an extra in a horror movie. I was assigned to the Acute Admissions ward, where the patients who were suffering most severely were admitted. These were seriously troubled individuals. I remember one man who had peculiar culinary tastes. Coming onto the ward one morning I noticed that all the heads were missing from a large bunch of tulips. He had eaten the lot. He was also fond of hard-boiled eggs, but ate them with the shells on! After smoking a cigarette, he would also eat the filter. I can't bring myself to do more than allude to his favourite kind of food, however. Let's just say he manufactured it himself!

Had it not been for the uniforms, it would have been hard to tell apart the staff from the patients. Some of the nurses on my ward were serious drinkers, and some also took drugs. I fitted in well.

The training I received helped me to understand myself a little better. Studying psychology and human biology, along with working with the patients, made me face up to the reality of where my life could actually lead – a similar hospital to the one I was working in, if not prison or the grave. But all the knowledge I was gaining still wasn't enough to stop me from slowly killing myself. I would crank up at home before going to work, and during tea or lunch breaks I would go out into the grounds to take more drugs.

During my early days of using drugs I had an acquaintance called Paddy. He was known as the life and soul of any party. You could never feel down when Paddy was around. Imagine my shock when he was admitted to my ward. He was exhibiting schizophrenic symptoms: auditory hallucinations – voices, to which he replied – and lapses into a catatonic state which rendered him immovable for days. These could be followed by manic outbursts which made him very aggressive.

Seeing Paddy on the ward made me panic. Although he was in a bad way, I could see that he recognised me. I knew that if I didn't get off that ward he might expose me in some way and I'd be in trouble. I quickly requested a few days' holiday, knowing that afterwards, my time on that particular ward would be over.

I began to compare myself with Paddy and ask myself some serious questions: *Will I ever be free of drugs? How can I get off them?* There didn't seem to be any answers – nothing new.

Eager to try anything that might help, I spotted an advert in the paper that said: *Are you stressed? Anxious? Do you want to give up smoking? Why not try Transcendental Meditation? It will effortlessly relieve your worries.*

This seemed too good to be true. I had to try it.

The classes were held in a local school hall. The sessions were run by a "guru" who told us that we needed to empty our minds and endlessly repeat a mantra that would help us. The aim was to open our minds to spiritual things. He told us to imagine what paradise and tranquillity were.

For a short time I tried to do this, but each time I left the safety of the school hall I smacked headfirst into reality again. I couldn't keep it up. I was told I had to meditate for half an hour each day. That was fine for people with time on their hands, but I had to crank up and work. I couldn't spare half an hour to get spaced out on fresh air.

As the months flew by my position on the ward became more senior as new junior nurses came into training. I sometimes did the "drug round", which was the highlight of my day. Although they were intended for the patients, I would slip a Largactil pill in my mouth (a major tranquiliser), together with an Artane tablet, which combatted the side effects of Largactil.

Whilst at the hospital I got on well with a nurse called Barbara. I discovered she was a Christian. She was always willing to lend a hand and was nothing short of an angel to the patients. She was able, by some feat unknown to the rest of us, to show each one genuine love and consideration. She scolded me for taking the micky out of them and treating them badly. But she was never stand-offish towards me. In fact, whenever she had the opportunity she would tell me about Jesus and my need of Him. Because she was very open about her faith, some of the other staff avoided Barbara, but I found her friendly and I drew close to her because I genuinely wanted to hear what she had to say.

One night, as I was walking through the town centre after coming off duty, I was picked up by the drugs squad. Drugs were now recognised as a huge problem in the community and the police were active in trying to clean up the streets before the situation got completely out of control. I was well known to them as a drugs offender and that night I just happened to be in the wrong place at the wrong time. Two policeman jumped out of a van and approached me.

"Oh look, it's Derbyshire – the drug head," one of them said.

"Yeah? What's the problem?" I replied cockily.

"You, you're the problem. Let's check and see what you've got on you."

I knew it was useless to protest. They spread-eagled me against the side of their van and did a body search.

"Found anything have you?" I asked, knowing full well that I was clean.

"No, but we're still taking you down to the station to give you a more thorough going over."

I couldn't do anything except go along with it. They put me in a cell and for the next few hours I sat and stared at the bare walls. I could hear a commotion going on in the next cell and strained to hear what was going on. Meanwhile, two police officers came into my cell and strip searched me. Finding nothing, they decided to give me a good hiding to repay my cockiness and began kicking me. One of them dropped his guard for a moment and I took the opportunity to hook him in the jaw. He crashed to the ground. That enraged them. They used me as a punch bag until they had vented their anger.

Whilst all this was going on, a guy I knew called Willy Davison was being put in the adjacent cell. This was the cause of the disturbance I'd been trying to figure out. Willy was a notorious Hell's Angel. Little did I know that the police had told him that I was in the next cell, and that I had grassed on him.

It was a few days later when I was smoking dope in my friend's flat, minding my own business, that Willy and his mates knocked at the door and came in. My friend and Willy had a hushed conversation in the corner, while I sat on the floor chilling out. I had no idea it had anything to do with me. I should have eavesdropped; I soon found out the truth.

"Hey, Darby!" Willy shouted.

I looked around to see his steel toe-capped boot flying towards my head. I made a snap decision. If I wanted to survive the inevitable beating, the best thing for me to do was take it and play dead. Willy laid into me and gave me what he thought I had coming. I was battered from head to foot. After he and his cohorts left, I tried to explain my innocence to my friend, but he wasn't interested. He just wanted me out of his flat.

I left. I could hardly walk. I couldn't possibly avenge myself in the state I was in. Willy might actually kill me for real. To try and tell him now that the police had fitted me up and that I'd never breathed a word about him to anyone would be useless. This situation just confirmed to me that I had to get off drugs and bury my current way of life before it buried me.

I decided I needed to create some distance between me and the local scene. Liverpool seemed like a fair distance away, so after I had managed to pass my exams and qualify – nothing short of a miracle – I moved there. I rented a flat in the Four Squares, which was a notoriously deprived area that has since been demolished and redeveloped. The Four Squares housing estate was like a war zone. The police were forever raiding houses and hauling people out of their homes in the early hours of the morning. Kids were stealing cars and breaking into people's houses like adults. When they had finished joy riding the cars they were usually dumped on the estate, which made the area look like a bomb site.

The residents also loved a good fight. One night, as I was coming home from work, I heard a whizzing sound and felt something sting me. I looked down and saw that my leg was covered with blood. I had been shot with an air rifle. I had to go back to the hospital to have the pellet removed.

The Toxteth area of Liverpool was where I scored drugs. I was vulnerable because I didn't know anyone and wasn't familiar with the scene. The fear of being ripped off or even killed never left me all the time I lived there. Work wasn't going too well either. I was disciplined because the quality of my work and my attitude weren't up to scratch. Physically I felt weak and I was slipping back into my old ways.

Whenever I visited my parents, which wasn't often, without fail my mum would say,

"Stephen, why don't you come home? You'll be better off here."

"No, Mum" I got tired of saying, "I'm alright where I'm living. Don't worry, I know what I'm doing."

Of course, I didn't, but I couldn't face being under the same roof as them. Back in Liverpool, though, a tight band of despair gripped me, smothering what little spark of life I had, so I made a decision. Stay in Liverpool and continue to go downhill, or move back home and hope for a better life. Reluctantly, I returned to my parents' house.

Mum and Dad were so happy to have me back home, but I found it hard as they constantly fussed over me. In return I gave them hell. Cheap wine was an inexpensive way of getting drunk, so I consumed a couple of bottles nearly every night, drinking them in between cranking up. It enabled me to keep relatively calm and together.

Out on the streets the drug situation was exploding. It was becoming increasingly difficult to get drugs and, in desperation, pushers were ripping off their customers. I had got in on the act too, selling any drugs that I could spare. Like so many, I cut the drugs with talc or icing sugar to make them go further.

Many hazards went with the territory of pushing. One night I was attacked by a gang of about ten men who had been lying in wait for me. I had been encroaching on someone else's territory. One guy took the lead and leapt at me. As I raised my arm to defend myself, he stabbed me with a Stanley knife. With so many assailants I thought my number was up but, seeing the blood pouring from my wound, the mob dispersed.

I managed to get myself to hospital. All the way there I reflected on how close to death I had come – *again*. I thought I might need more than stitches, perhaps a blood transfusion. But after the doctor had examined me he told me that it was a superficial wound and all I needed was a bandage and a tetanus injection.

Life at home with Mum and Dad gradually became more tolerable. Dad never gave up telling me about Jesus. Instead of getting annoyed about it, like I had before, I started to listen in a half-hearted way. He told me that he was praying for me. He also said that they had a new pastor at his church – David Tinnion – a young guy who understood young people. Dad suggested I might go along with him one day and see for myself.

"You're joking, Dad. Me and church don't agree with each other."

"But lad, you could just try it."

"No thanks, Dad. I'm happy as I am."

During the summer months the church organised days out together. One day they were going to the Lake District and my parents asked if I wanted to join them. Normally I would have laughed off the suggestion of a day spent in the company of a bunch of Christians, but recently I had been reading the Bible in secret – a psalm here and there and a few verses from the New Testament. Maybe Dad's persistence was having an effect on me. I couldn't fully understand what I was reading, but something encouraged me to keep returning to it.

In addition, I had begun reading biographies of people whose lives had been changed by God. I not only enjoyed them, but I was impressed by how their lives had been turned around. Once there was no hope for them, now there was.

I agreed to go with my parents and the trip to the Lakes turned out to be great fun. A number of young people went and I got along really well with a guy called Mike Wilson. He knew all about me, which made me feel at ease, and he chatted easily with me about everyday things – which convinced me that he wasn't out of touch with life like some of the Christians I'd met in the past. He was football mad too, just like me, so we really hit it off.

That day I realised something very important: these young people were experiencing something exhilarating that was far beyond anything I had injected, snorted, smoked or drunk. Now was as good a time as any to change my way of living. If I left it any longer, it might be too late.

So it was that one Sunday night I voluntarily accompanied my parents to church. They were so pleased. My stomach was churning over and over as nervous anticipation flooded through me. I had to face the fact that there was only one way to start a new page in the history of my life. I had tried everything under the sun and nothing else had worked. Mr Hesketh, out of the kindness of his heart, had done everything he could for me. But all the goodwill and work of social workers, doctors and nurses, clinics and even the police hadn't stopped me from abusing drugs and suffering the consequences of the life that accompanied them. Deep down I sensed that God alone had the power to change my life. If He couldn't, then no one else could and an early death beckoned. I was banking on Him.

Just inside the door of the church people greeted my parents, who in turn introduced me. I felt a bit like a pedigree dog on show, but I sensed the people were well meaning, so I didn't take offence. We sat about half way down the church hall and I noticed there were only about half a dozen or so young people in attendance. My chair felt uncomfortable and I began to fidget.

The need to crank up was growing, but I was determined to get through the service and find out if God could do anything for me.

The service began with a song. People stood up and began clapping. This was new to me. The last time I had been in a church the only sign of life was the birds singing outside. When the song ended, a few people got up and began telling everyone how they became a Christian. None of them had gone through my experience, but I could identify with what they were saying. Their lives had been empty and unfulfilled before accepting Jesus.

Then the pastor, David Tinnion, got up to speak. I can't remember most of what he said, but one phrase cut me deeply:

"If you were the only person in the world, Jesus would still have died for you."

As this truth hit home, tears pricked my eyes. I couldn't hold them back. I felt ashamed of myself as different episodes from my life flashed through my mind. A huge mountain of guilt began to weigh heavily on my shoulders. I was overwhelmed with emotion, drowning in the knowledge of how terrible my life was and what a complete mess I'd made of it.

At the end of his sermon David asked if there was anyone who wanted to give their life to Christ. Silence hung over the gathering and it seemed that most people had their heads bowed. Mine was too, but that was because I was being torn apart. I wanted to scream out and run to the altar, throw myself down and beg for God's forgiveness. But I felt as though strong, invisible arms were gripping me like a vice, holding me back from responding to David's question.

"Help me, God!" I cried silently. "Help me!"

My breathing became laboured and I felt like I was suffocating. I desperately needed God's forgiveness – not only for my drug abuse and the sordid lifestyle that went with it, but also for my rejection of Jesus. Of its own volition my arm slowly rose into the air. I wanted Jesus.

That moment, when I raised my hand, signalled that my decision was made and my struggling was over. God's love flowed over me like a waterfall. Suddenly, amazingly, remorse, shame and a host of other feelings were swept away and replaced with acceptance. I knew, without any words being spoken, that God in His greatness and mercy, had received me and that I was cleansed and forgiven.

Words fail me at this point to try and explain what had taken place inside me. Mere words cannot do justice to the fact that the God who created all things, and has power over all things, had performed major heart surgery on me, Stephen Derbyshire, in spite of all I had done in the past. He wanted me. Now I was His.

In the background I could hear people crying. I was the only person to come to Christ that night. Some of the people in the church knew my history and had been faithfully praying for me. Their prayers had been answered.

After the meeting, as was customary in the church when dealing with new Christians, I was taken into a small room to be counselled. With all due respect, that nearly ruined the whole evening for me. For instance, I was told that I would have to give up smoking straight away. And as for the drugs, all that would have to go immediately too. When the counsellors went on to pray for me, I just wanted to run out of the door; to put as much distance between me and them as possible.

It reminded me of the time when some well-meaning Christians had visited the hospital where I was recovering from my operation. They offered to pray for me and I thought, "Well, it can't do any harm," so I said yes. But, instead of communicating God's love to me they laid hands on me and began to pray to cast out the "demons of drug addiction, smoking and drinking". It frightened the life out of me. I wanted to get out of my bed and leg it, but they were actually holding me down. Then, when they began speaking in tongues, I thought they were psychotic and in need of more help than me.

What I wanted to know now was, if God had accepted me for who I was, then why did these people want to change me? Surely that was God's job.

I told Mum and Dad that I wanted to walk home alone that evening. I had a lot to think about. I reflected on the events of the night. I had definitely met with God. No one could ever convince me otherwise. I had the clear sense that Jesus was now in control of my life and the peace that came with this knowledge was a better "high" than any drug had ever given me.

Mum was making a pot of tea when I arrived home. She looked at me and asked if I wanted some. Dad appeared in the kitchen and tentatively asked how I was. I could see they were both restraining themselves from probing too deeply, both holding down their excitement.

"Alright, lad?"

"Yeah, fine Dad."

I asked him for a Bible, which he gladly provided, and I took it up to my room. Questions flooded my mind and I had a crisis of doubt. "How am I going to tell my friends what has happened to me? What about cold turkey?"

The voice of the enemy sowed further doubt:

"Where will God be when your muscles start to cramp up and you start hallucinating – seeing insects crawling all over you? Where will your Jesus be then?"

The voice of my own doubt provided the answer: *you're on your own, Darby.*

By the time this barrage of doubt, fear and unbelief had left me I was exhausted. I wondered if indeed I was actually a Christian. Past incidents kept coming up in my mind and I felt that I was just too bad to be accepted by God. I was a junkie and that would be me until the day I died. A real battle took place in my bedroom that night, but God was in control…

I woke up bleary eyed the next morning and sat up in bed. The desire to crank up – which had been my daily experience for years – had gone. That was when I knew for sure that God was with me. It was utterly incredible. That morning I got up, washed and dressed, and went for a walk in the park. It was the first time in years that I had not had to take drugs simply to get me out of bed. Incredible!

Walking through the park that morning I felt like I had entered a new world. My negative thinking cleared and I was able to appreciate creation – the grass and trees, the birdsong drifting through the air. The sky appeared a brilliant blue. I was overcome by emotion, caught up in the ecstasy of the moment. I cried and cried like I had never done before.

I never once experienced cold turkey. Days later I still didn't have the urge to take drugs and there wasn't a twinge of withdrawal. God had seen to all of that.

The day that I went back to work I was a new Stephen Derbyshire. Where once I would have been cold and dismissive towards the patients, probably treating them quite harshly, I now felt a new compassion towards them and made a point of being kind and considerate.

I told Barbara what had happened to me and she was absolutely delighted. She overflowed with thanks to God for saving me. She told me that she had been praying for me for a long time and was grateful that He had answered her.

I was consumed by the fact that my life had been given back to me, so I didn't want to waste another moment of it – and I didn't want anyone else to waste theirs, either. So straight away I began telling others what God had done for me. It was a disaster!

I thought I would start with my Charge Nurse, who was a Jehovah's Witness. I told him what had happened to me and hoped that he would ask Jesus into his life. No chance. He responded by baffling me with his interpretation of various Bible verses and told me that what I had experienced was of the devil; that I should go along to his Kingdom Hall in order to find God.

I was flabbergasted. How could he, or anyone else, suggest that my experience was not genuine? How could anyone reject what I knew God had done for me? The evidence was plain to see. No one else had been able to get me off drugs after years of persistence and many different approaches. But God had accomplished it in one night – and with no side effects!

I decided to go and see Mr Hesketh. I hoped that surely he would understand. I told him my story and sat back to see his reaction. Understandably, he was a bit sceptical at first. I guess he suspected that whatever I'd experienced was just another flash in the pan; that soon I would get over it and be back to shooting up and hanging out with the other addicts.

One night on the ward I recognised a face from the past. It was one of the teachers from my old secondary school. Apparently he'd had a nervous breakdown and needed hospitalisation – on my ward, of all places.

Without further ado, I told him about Jesus. He could not get over the shock of seeing me with my life together, after all the mayhem I'd caused at school. And a Christian too? Surely not! He told me that my old Head, Mr Watts, would be coming in to see him, and that when he did he would give me a shout to let me know.

This happened in due course. On the day that Mr Watts turned up at the hospital I was sporting a large, bright green badge which said, "Jesus Loves You". Mr Watts just couldn't comprehend that I, Stephen Derbyshire, the terror of Central Comprehensive School, the lad who would "never be any good", was now a nurse and a Christian.

I told him about Jesus and in return he told me that I had been the worst pupil he'd had in 20 years! But as a result of our meeting, he later invited me into the school to talk to the pupils about my life then and now, since accepting Jesus.

As I spoke to more and more people about the difference Jesus had made in my life, the truths I was learning about God really sank in. I read my Bible regularly and now I wouldn't miss church for the world. My relationship with my parents improved 100%, especially with Dad. We became great friends. My sister Norma, however, couldn't understand what all the fuss was about. This Jesus business was too much for her, although she couldn't deny the change in me. She didn't become a Christian until ten years later.

I really had become a new person. My old life seemed light years behind me, as though someone else had lived it. Such is the quality of God's grace. I liked to spend time alone with God in my room, reading His word. Even though there was much of it that I didn't understand, just reading the words did something for me.

A few months into my Christian life I was reflecting on how much God had changed my circumstances. I was filled with gratitude – so much so that I couldn't really express it in words. How could I repay God for all He had done for me? Of course, I realised there was nothing I could do; nothing I could give God in exchange for His goodness. Yet I had a huge desire to do something for Him. Late one night, after I had been reading the

Scriptures, I talked with God before I fell asleep and said,

"Lord, for the rest of my time on this earth, I promise that I will always follow you."

7
FROM THE OLD TO THE NEW

The man standing on the stage spoke.

"I've been a Christian for twelve months now and my life has really changed."

It was Norman Barrett who was speaking, lead guitarist for the band *The Gravy Train*. He was the guest speaker at the local YMCA. I liked his band and had bought their records before I became a Christian, so I was intrigued. From what Norman said, it sounded as though our lives were quite similar.

The event had been organised so that Christians could bring along their non-Christian friends. About 400 people were there, having a good time and listening to the music. Amid the smoking and chatting the message about Jesus was being preached. I thought it was fabulous. I wanted to get onto the platform myself to say a few words of encouragement. But, when I looked around at all those faces in the crowd, I knew that I would have been reduced to a bag of nerves. Talking to crowds of people was definitely not me.

During the interval I went to get myself a cup of tea and spotted some people I knew from my previous way of life. I made a beeline for them, bursting to tell them all about Jesus and what He had done for me, but at the same time nervous about doing so. Norman Barrett had said a few words about overcoming your shyness in order to tell others about God, so I took some courage from that and approached them.

"Hi" I said.

"Darby! Nice to see you. How are you doing?"

"Fine, how are you?"

"OK" came a chorus of replies.

"What do you make of what that guy said, Darby?" one of them asked.

This was my golden opportunity. I sent up a silent prayer of thanks to God.

"Well, what Norman said is right, you know," I began. "Jesus can change you if you ask Him into your life. I did and now I hardly recognise myself."

I was smiling broadly, glad that I had done it. I had managed to speak to some people who already knew what I was like.

There was a pregnant pause. It can only have been seconds, but it felt like an hour. Then they all burst out laughing.

"Ha! You're having us on!"

"Oh no," I thought. "They don't believe me."

I wondered what I should do. I didn't know how to handle the situation.

"It's true," I said.

With that they began firing questions at me. The usual kind of questions that die-hard sceptics ask; the kind of things I would have said not that long ago.

"If God's real, why is there so much suffering in the world? Why are so many kids around the world homeless or being abused or starving to death? What's the answer to that, Darby?"

My mouth was dry. I couldn't think of what to say. I tried to put a brave face on it.

"All that's got nothing to do with God," I said. I was out of my depth and I knew it.

"All this stuff is rubbish, Darby," someone else said. "Do you really believe that Jesus rose from the dead?"

Back on more solid ground I replied, "Yes, I do – and He did."

"No way, you've lost it Darby. You're going mad."

One of them pulled out a pack of cigarettes and stuck one in his mouth.

"You got a light, Darby?"

I responded before I thought about what I was saying – and it wasn't the most tactful response I'd ever given.

"Listen, if you don't receive Jesus as your Saviour, where you're going to end up you won't need matches, you'll be surrounded by flames!"

It didn't go down well. I slunk back to my seat. "Who do they think they are, talking about Jesus like that?" I thought to myself. "Look what He's done for me." Then I remembered that I had been just like them, only a lot worse. "Sorry Lord," I prayed. "I shouldn't have spoken to them like that."

Glancing up I spotted my old friend Frank, from the holiday club. The last time I'd seen him was on the night when me and my friends had gone mad in the Fishnet Club and Pip Wilson had thrown us out. My face and neck felt flushed with embarrassment. Frank was standing with a group of people, so I didn't know whether to go over and speak to him or not. But my legs seemed to have a will of their own and the next thing I knew I was standing beside him.

"Hi Frank."

Frank looked at me, squinting.

"Darby?"

"Yes, it's me." I smiled. "I've become a Christian."

We shook hands and the surprise on his face was clear to see.

"That's fantastic, Steve," he said. "Praise God!"

He quickly wrapped up his conversation with the people he was with, then guided me to a quiet corner so we could chat uninterrupted.

"Tell me, Steve. How are you doing? How have you found living the faith?"

First I told him how I had become a Christian, and then what I was experiencing now. I was glad that he asked me, because he knew my background and must have realised it would be a tough transition from cranking up to becoming a Christian.

As I told him how I was feeling, it felt as though a great weight lifted off my shoulders. I explained about the doubts that sometimes blocked my thinking, even though I knew that God had forgiven me and wiped the slate clean.

Of course, only I could know what was happening deep inside me. I was a changed person in every way. Now, if I did something wrong, like shouting at my mum, I would feel very bad about it and apologise at once. Before I would have shouted her down, not thinking twice about it, and would have felt no remorse.

I understood the extent to which God had changed me the day that a patient deliberately spat in my face at the hospital. The old Darby would have retaliated immediately and violently. But after the initial surge of adrenalin, I said a few calm words to the guy then wiped my face. I had certainly changed.

Foul language used to punctuate every other word I spoke. I did it without even thinking. Now, however, I was aware of my words and their impact. I still swore at times, but now, incredibly, my language was seasoned with grace. At times I was still afraid that maybe I wouldn't make it as a Christian – that I'd lapse back into my old life – but I knew that Jesus was the only answer to all my needs. Without Him in my life I would be finished.

One thing that was a conundrum and a frustration to me was

smoking. God had supernaturally taken away my craving for drugs, but He hadn't done the same with my smoking. I prayed that He would, but for some reason He wasn't answering my prayers. When I did smoke, I felt guilty about it, and my mind was plagued by the disapproval of others – which, perversely, made me smoke all the more. As each Sunday service drew to a close I would begin to squirm in my seat, hoping it would wind up quickly so that I could run outside and light up. I felt that it was wrong, but I couldn't help it and still liked the calming effect that having a cigarette had on me.

I couldn't bring myself to tell anyone else about these concerns. I'd tried that in the past and had a load of Bible verses quoted at me, which I didn't fully understand, like my body being a temple of the Holy Spirit. It hadn't helped me at all. Which is why it was a big relief to now be able to offload all of this to Frank.

Frank kept silent and listened to all I had to say. Then he reassured me that everything I was going through was part of the process of growing and being built up in the faith. God doesn't reach out of the sky and hand us everything on a plate, Frank explained. He moves by His Spirit and expects us to trust Him to bring us through.

I told Frank that I'd heard a lot of Christian language being spoken that I didn't understand. To me it was completely baffling and confusing.

"Someone told me that I needed to be washed in the blood of the Lamb," I said. It had frightened me to death. Initially I thought I must have accidentally walked into a cult with some kind of weird initiation rite. But when it was explained to me, I was still none the wiser. Frank laughed.

"It's just Christian terminology," he said. "Nothing for you to worry about right now."

I wasn't entirely convinced by Frank urging me not to worry, but just being able to share my doubts and concerns with him was so helpful. Then Frank gave me a bit of news about how God had moved him on.

"I'm now the verger of St Nicholas," he told me. "They've given me a house and in the next few weeks I'll be holding a series of Bible studies for new Christians called The Navigators. Why don't you come along to that?"

It's amazing the difference God can make to a person's life. I knew Frank. I knew his background in drink and drugs. But now God had changed him. He had become a respectable man in the community and a positive role model for me. I told him I'd love to come to the Bible studies.

Back in my seat the concert continued and I enjoyed it all the more, knowing that God had provided a way for me to get off my chest all the things that were bothering me. I also now had something to look forward to – the Bible studies with Frank and other new Christians. I felt that this would really help me to hang on to God.

The Bible study evenings turned out to be brilliant. I loved them. Frank was a very good communicator. I had loads of questions, but Frank was able to answer them in a way that I could understand.

Some of the people at the meetings had been Christians for a while and others, like me, were new believers. There the similarity stopped because everyone appeared to have been straight (non-drug users) in the past. This made me apprehensive about telling them my story of coming to Jesus, in case they freaked out, or worse, rejected me. I told Frank about my worries. He reassured me that everyone has a story to tell about their lives before Christ. Not one of us is perfect. That's the reason Jesus died for our sins.

God doesn't grade sin according to its severity. Sin is sin. There are no minor or major sins. Before Jesus we were all in darkness, but He brought us into the light.

Even though I knew Frank was speaking the truth, I still held back from sharing my testimony. I also had a bit of a problem with praying out loud. Just as some Christians spoke using terminology that was not easily understood, this carried over into their praying. As soon as some people began to pray, they suddenly turned into Shakespeare, peppering their speech with "thees" and "thous". I couldn't pray like that. I just wanted to use ordinary, everyday words when I spoke to the Lord.

Day by day, despite my problems, I began to get a real sense of who God is and what He meant to me. When I talked to Him I knew, without a shadow of a doubt, that He was listening. I knew that He was my Father and cared for me. God was for me, not against me. He wasn't someone holding a big stick over my head, waiting for me to make a mistake, so that He could lash out at me. He was bigger than any of my wrongdoings and His love for me was ultimately revealed in the person of Jesus.

My desire to know God grew and grew. I wanted more of Him in my life. If someone had told me six months prior to my coming to faith in Jesus that this is how I'd be living my life – and enjoying every minute of it – I would have laughed at them. In fact, I'd have probably beaten them up. But here I was, completely hungry to know God.

Meeting Pip Wilson again further encouraged my faith. I saw him at a Youth For Christ meeting and when I told him I had become a Christian he was absolutely delighted. He spoke positively about how my life could only get better and better.

I loved going to church and became actively involved. When they planned to hold a week-long youth outreach I wanted to do all I could to help. At the end of a week of evangelism the film *The Cross and the Switchblade* would be shown and I had been asked to speak about what Jesus had done in my life. The idea of standing up and speaking in front of a large crowd of people was, frankly, terrifying. I wanted to do it, but fears and doubts plagued my mind and I wasn't sure I could pull it off.

That week, being part of a small evangelistic team, armed with leaflets and tracts, was a new thing for me. But I wanted people to be able to know Jesus the same way that I did. I concluded that if they wouldn't come to church, then I needed to go out onto the streets to tell them about Him. Then, hopefully, they too would come to church.

The only aspect of street evangelism that concerned me was running into my old friends. Hardened junkies were going to be hard work to talk to. I imagined talking to the likes of Benny or Willy Davison – especially if they happened to be out of their heads at the time. Benny would probably laugh his head off and ask me what I was on, so that he could have some. As for Willy, I imagined that he would want to carry on where he'd left off and try to kick me to death.

For all my reservations, however, Saturday morning found me standing in the same shopping centre that had been a regular rendezvous point for obtaining drugs. There I was, handing out leaflets and trying to get into conversation with shoppers who either ignored me or took a leaflet and promptly threw it away.

After a couple of hours of getting nowhere and feeling uptight, I prayed, "Lord, where are all the people you want me to talk to?" God had given me the desire to go out onto the streets in the first place. It seemed logical that He must therefore have someone He wanted me to speak to.

God sent His answer, just not in the way I expected. In the

distance I spotted a gang of my former friends spilling out of The Market, a pub we used to frequent. They were headed towards me and I could see by their demeanour that they were stoned.

My first instinct was to run away. My eyes darted around looking for somewhere to hide. There was nowhere obvious. I had planted myself in the middle of a large, open space, with the shops some distance away. There was no escape. My stomach began to churn. I wanted God to make me disappear!

"Lord, can we do a deal?" I pleaded earnestly. "If they go out of their way to come over to me, I'll tell them about you. If they head away from me, I'll save what I have to say to them for another day."

A clear sign came. I wandered a bit off my spot, towards the shops, away from my friends. But it was like they were magnetically attracted to me, altering their course so that they were headed right for me. I knew God was going to get me to talk to them. The confidence I'd set out with that morning vanished like mist. They got closer so I feigned interest in whatever was in the nearest shop window, pretending not to see them.

I could see them reflected in the glass. My heart sank still further as I noticed that one of the group was a guy known as "Alibob". He was the original nutter, nothing but trouble. He was clearly wasted. *Why him of all people?* I thought. *He's got such a big mouth.*

I closed my eyes, but then came a tap on my shoulder.

"Darby? Is that you?"

Reluctantly I turned around. I was gripping my jumper, hoping and praying that the bunch of leaflets I'd just stuffed under it wouldn't fall out.

"Hi, Alibob," I replied feebly.

"Is there something we should know, eh, Darby?" he said

too loudly. "Are you buying ladies underwear or have you gone freaky?"

I shot a glance over my shoulder. The window I had supposedly been intently looking into was a fancy lingerie boutique! A lie quickly rolled off my tongue.

"Well, I, err .. I was looking for something for my mum, for her birthday."

"You're a right liar, Darby" boomed Alibob. Everyone burst out laughing. To add insult to injury, I momentarily forgot that I was hiding the leaflets and, at that inopportune moment, they all came tumbling out and scattered on the pavement.

A couple of my friends bent down to help me pick them up. One of the lads, Shawie, began to read aloud the words on the leaflet.

"Jesus can change your life … what's this load of rubbish Darby?"

It's now or never, I told myself.

"Like it says, Jesus can change your life if you'll let Him."

Alibob turned to the others and bellowed,

"He's lost the plot guys!"

"No, it's true," I repeated. "God makes a difference to everyone's life if they let Him."

"Darby, listen to me man," Alibob said. "If you want to score, I've got some good stuff on me. Give me a couple of quid if that's all you've got and it's yours. I can see you're in a bad way." He touched my arm.

"No, you don't understand," I said. "I don't need it anymore. I've found someone who has filled the gap in my life that I tried to fill with drugs. His name is Jesus. He's become my whole life. I'm telling you, it's true."

I spoke quietly but with conviction. The words flowed out and my friends were silent. *Thank you, God* I prayed inwardly, *they're actually listening.* I knew it was entirely down to Him, not my doing. As I continued to speak they gazed at me through hazy, drugged eyes, as though struggling to decipher my words.

"Come along this evening," I encouraged them, "and see this great film we're showing. Afterwards I'm going to talk about how I was able to give up drugs and become a Christian."

I wasn't sure if I would see them that evening or not. I knew that they were firmly in the grip of hard drugs.

* * *

That evening, I was sitting on the front row of the church. It was one of the hardest days of my life. I kept turning around, seeing the church filling up until it was completely packed. A few people were having to stand at the back, it was so full. One of the stewards rushed up to David, our pastor, and said that someone was smoking at the back of the hall. He got up and followed him to sort it out. I hoped it wasn't one of my friends.

Sitting alone, my thoughts tumbling, I was worried that I would ruin the whole evening; that I would be struck dumb, paralysed with fear. So far I had seen both Mr Hesketh, my probation officer, and Mr Watts, my old headmaster come in, but I hadn't spoken to either of them. I preferred to leave that until afterwards, if I got through it alright. Then I'd have something to talk to them about.

A few of the friends I'd met in the afternoon had turned up after all. I could see them sitting to one side of me, talking among themselves. I was encouraged by this and decided to direct my words mainly to them, in the hope that they would understand where I was coming from and respond to God.

It was planned that as soon as the film finished, I would get up and begin speaking. I had been practicing my speech in front of the bathroom mirror for days. It took exactly 20 minutes – I'd timed it. When I was introduced I found it difficult to stand up. Then, when I got in position and looked at the sea of faces, my head swam; I wanted to pass out. It was probably only a second, but seemed like an eternity. I looked at the faces I knew so well – my parents, my friends, members of the church.

I began to speak. My well rehearsed 20-minute speech was all over in 5 minutes. Afterwards I slumped heavily back into my chair, beads of sweat running down my face. I wanted to throw up and cry. I had messed it up. I felt as though I'd lost control of my voice when I spoke, and I was distracted by the echoes bouncing off the walls. All the things that I'd really wanted to say had fled my mind and the words that came out were not the ones I'd planned. *Never again*, I told myself. I could speak to people one on one, or a couple at a time, but in front of a crowd was too much for me. Leave that to the Billy Grahams of the world.

But when David gave the appeal for those who wanted to give their lives to Christ, I was stunned to see quite a number of people come forward. Later several people came to me and said that if God could change me, He could change them too. At first I thought they were just saying it to make me feel better after my disastrous speech, but as the evening continued, I wondered if I had really got it wrong after all.

Mr Watts came over and congratulated me. He didn't seem to have been touched by the message, but he said that he thought Jesus had done me the world of good and that pleased him. When Mr Hesketh spoke to me, I knew that he could see something in me that confirmed the truth of all I'd been telling him – that Jesus had changed my life. He told me that he saw an enormous difference in me. He didn't respond to the appeal either, but asked if I would go around and see him during the week. A few days later when I saw him, Mr Hesketh asked if I would be prepared to go into prisons and tell the inmates about my life and how I had changed. I said that it would be a great privilege.

Although I'd been embarrassed and felt as though I'd made a mess, actually the whole evening had been a success. David asked me if I'd like to give my testimony again when the church was holding another outreach. All the positive feedback I'd received had boosted my confidence a lot, so I was up for it. God had proved to me that He was working things out in my life. Now He was beginning to use me in ways I would never have thought possible.

Mr Hesketh arranged for me to take a short course in counselling. When I had completed it I was eager to start work and he sent me to visit prisoners in Strangeways and Risley – the very prison where I'd been on remand. I worked in the juvenile wing with prisoners who were a little younger than me. The prison officers were wary of me, as they knew I was an ex-con and didn't understand what I was trying to do. Some of the inmates didn't respond to me too well either.

A guy called Jeremy was one of the first people I spent time counselling. He was a punk rocker and Sid Vicious was his idol. He was in for drug-related offences and acts of violence. He was tall and thin and had all the hallmarks of a drug user. He expected to be sentenced to about a year, so accepting and settling into prison life seemed to him to be the best thing to do. On my third visit I told him about how I had taken drugs for years and reached a stage where I wanted to come off, but couldn't. Only Jesus was able to sort me out. Jeremy appeared to be listening and taking it all in, but I wasn't sure.

Between that visit and the next, the church prayed for him. When I visited him again, Jeremy started to open up and he told me about his life, which was similar to mine. I hoped he would become a Christian there and then, but he didn't. When he was finally released he did come to church. I was absolutely thrilled and welcomed him like the father in the parable of the prodigal son. The congregation had never seen anything like Jeremy, with his spiky green hair, tight black jeans, safety pins all over his body and what seemed like dozens of earrings in his earlobes and one through his nose.

Jeremy came to church a few times and one evening, as we prayed together, he asked Jesus into his life. I was jubilant. Sadly, however, it didn't last. Jeremy's friends were constantly calling round his house and one night he decided to go out with them and got stoned. This resulted in him getting into trouble, reoffending, and being sent back to prison.

Of the prisons I visited, I preferred Strangeways over Risley, which held bad memories for me. Also, the prisoners in Strangeways had already been sentenced, so they opened up more quickly and were more truthful than Risley's inmates. Strangeways had been built in the year dot and was old, smelly and depressing. It made me appreciate Jesus all the more. I could easily have ended up there myself.

Throughout the year that I worked there, I saw a number of prisoners and we met in a room on the wing, spending about two hours talking. I enjoyed seeing them and felt that they too looked forward to my visits. I did wonder whether my visit simply broke the monotony for them, as they were normally only allowed one visit per month.

I developed strong relationships with the men I spoke to. They told me personal things about their lives: how they worried about their wives and children; how they feared coping with their sentences without going mad or doing something crazy. I listened to all their concerns and prayed for them after each visit.

Tony, who was about the same age as me, had been imprisoned for violence. He came from a nightmarish background and his lifestyle and subsequent conviction were all wrapped up in it. Ideally, the church should have been able to offer men like these refuge and support until they were strong enough to get back on their feet, but we couldn't. I hoped this would change in the future.

One cold winter's morning I asked Tony if he wanted to know God more. He said that he did, and there and then he asked Jesus into his life. We had an amazing time praying and worshipping God together. The small room where we met was filled with God's presence and after that, each time we met it was very encouraging for us both. Tony too came to church after he was released, but not long afterwards he drifted away and we lost contact.

Although on the surface it seemed as though people were coming to God one minute and turning away from Him the next, this didn't deter me at all. God was in control and He alone knew what was going on in their lives. God continued to encourage me to tell others about Him and I did.

Life for me still had its ups and downs. Becoming a Christian doesn't mean that instantly everything changes that needs to change, and neither are we immune from life's troubles. Living in Christ is a gradual, growing process. Sometimes it's a struggle. I found it hard to hold on, keep praying and keep reading my Bible. At other times, when I needed Him most, God showed up in His power.

I was still working at Rainhill Hospital and one day a man was admitted to my ward to recover from alcohol dependence. We nursed him in a side room where he was given Heminevrin (a type of tranquiliser) to help him dry out. We would take his blood pressure hourly to make sure that no complications arose. One day, as I opened his door, I could see him writhing like a snake in his bed. He was moaning and crying for someone to help him. It was pitiful. As I stood there, suddenly a sharp pain hit me in the stomach. Immediately I began to shake and sweat profusely. It was like experiencing cold turkey – all the symptoms were there. I went straight to the Ward Sister and told her I had the flu coming on and needed to go home.

Halfway there I decided that home wasn't the best place to be, so instead I turned the car around and headed for the countryside. I pulled over in a country lane, grabbed my Bible, and climbed out in a daze, determined to seek the Lord. All along I felt very strongly that I wasn't experiencing the real thing; it was the devil trying to attack me, trying to lure me back into his grasp.

"God, help me!" I cried out as I walked. "Help me, Lord. I can't take this pressure."

The cold turkey symptoms disappeared as suddenly as they had come. I began to praise God. Again, He had revealed His strength and power to me, an ordinary man.

I found that God directed me to spend more time with my old circle of friends. He gave me the courage to speak to them on their own ground. I would hang out with them in the town centre, sitting on the benches with them, telling them about Jesus. Or I would go and visit them in their run down, stinking squats and spend time encouraging them to give up their way of life and come to God. They also used to hang around a particular café, so I would spend quite a few afternoons there, speaking to them about God.

One afternoon I was chatting with a group in the café when in walked Alex. My heart sank. I knew him only too well from the drug scene. I had hated him then, and I wasn't too thrilled to see him now. I knew him to be flash, cocky and a regular big mouth, but his real reputation was for ripping people off as a pusher.

As I was busy explaining the gospel to a small group of people around a table, Alex came over and butted into our conversation. I ignored him at first, which wasn't easy, and carried on talking to the others. Then he said,

"Watch this lads, I'll get Darby."

I pretended I hadn't heard him and carried on.

"Hey Darby," he said loudly, "I've read in that Bible of yours that God said if someone hits you, you're supposed to turn the other cheek and get smacked in the mouth again. Isn't that true?"

I had to answer him. "Yeah."

Without another word he hit me. But instead of turning the other cheek, I immediately knocked him to the floor. As I pulled back my fist to punch him again though, a strong sense of guilt swept over me. Instead, I stretched out my hand to help him up and said,

"I'm sorry, would you forgive me?"

Shakily he stood to his feet, stared at me, then walked off.

I felt that my whole Christian life had gone up in smoke with that one punch. How could I now turn around and tell these people that Jesus loved them after I'd just smacked Alex in the mouth?! Then it dawned on me. Jesus had changed me. I spoke to the group I was with:

"Look, I'm really sorry I hit him like that. But God has changed me. If he'd done that before I became a Christian I wouldn't have stopped at one punch. I'd have beaten him to a pulp and thought nothing of it. But that way of life has now gone. God is changing me bit by bit. It's understandable if I still react that way sometimes."

They agreed. Mainly, I suspected, because they thought Alex deserved it. However, I learned from this experience that although I would make many mistakes, God would teach me valuable lessons from them, helping me to trust Him more. The way in which I handle things now is vastly different from then, of course. Christ is that difference.

The local police, especially the drugs squad, were very active around this time as drugs were a major menace in the area. Anyone connected with them, past or present, was always under suspicion. The police simply didn't believe that I was a changed person and quite frequently I would be picked up, searched, questioned, and sometimes hauled into the police station.

It was a regular custom in St Helens to welcome in the New Year in the town hall square. I had just attended the Watch Night service and was passing through the square on my way home. A man was suspended from one of the hands of the town hall clock, like a scene from *Back To The Future*, and this seemed to stir up a kind of lunacy in the crowd. Everyone went wild. I was simply caught up in the fray, unable to get away, but the police grabbed and arrested me.

At the police station I was spread-eagled against a wall and searched, but instead of finding drugs they found my Bible.

"What's this, eh?" came the surprised question.

"It's a Bible. I'm a Christian," I replied calmly.

They ignored this and continued to ask me questions about what drugs I was on and who was dealing in what. The more I told them I no longer had any interest in drugs, the more they questioned me.

Finally they accepted what I was saying and one of them said, "I've never met anyone like you before, who's been converted." I spoke to them about Jesus and told one officer, who I'd met many times before, that he needed Christ.

"Why?" he asked.

"Because you're a miserable old so-and-so," I said.

He laughed and released me to go home.

By now the whole town knew that I'd become a Christian. Word had spread and people would stop me in the street to ask me about my faith and how it affected my life.

My dad was thrilled with the change in me. We now got on so well that no one would ever have believed the trouble I caused him and Mum. He encouraged my faith and we had many long conversations, not just about the Bible but everyday things. Similarly, my mum had a permanent smile on her face. The years of long, hard prayers had paid off.

My close friends from my old life changed their attitude towards me. At first they thought I'd lost it and gone mad. Then they tried to avoid me. Now they realised the change was for real and this gained me their respect. Whenever I saw them I would ask how they were. I felt genuine concern for them and would tell them about Jesus. From where I now stood, I could see the drugs were eating them up. They were deteriorating before my eyes. Often I would weep at the tragedy of their situation. My offer of guiding them to the help that only Jesus could provide was very attractive to some of them, but the drugs had them in a stranglehold.

I often visited the Christian bookshop in town. I used to buy tracts there to give away to people. The lady who ran the shop knew me well and one Saturday afternoon she phoned me at home to say that someone was in the shop asking for me.

"Who is it?" I wondered.

"He says his name is John and that he's a friend of yours."

"OK, tell him I'll be right over."

When I got there, John, otherwise known as Twink, was bombed out of his head. His speech was slurred and he was staggering all over the place, bumping into displays and knocking into other customers. He was talking, but I couldn't understand a word he was saying.

I got Twink into my car and drove him into the countryside. He was weeping and telling me that he desperately wanted to come off drugs. He knew they would kill him and he didn't want to die. He had heard what had happened to me and he wanted Christ in his life.

I prayed with him and told him, "Twink, you've got to get yourself straight. I'll take you home now and tomorrow I'll come and pick you up and we'll go from there."

The next day I went to see him in the Salvation Army hostel where he was staying and we talked for hours about the Lord. Soon after this he became a Christian. Twink loved the Lord – there was no doubt about that – and he became very active in the church. But from time to time he wrestled with drugs. It seemed as though as soon as he had made it through a bad patch, it would start all over again.

Despite this we had good times of fellowship together and sometimes joined forces to do evangelism amongst our friends. Twink was one of the first people I'd led to the Lord who remained a Christian. Sadly, Twink also had diabetes, which always got out of control whenever he was having problems and after about ten years he died. I was grateful that at least he passed away knowing the Lord.

Another of my friends who became a Christian was Paul – the guy at the party who had held up the crucifix. I bumped into him one Saturday in the town centre.

"Darby," he said. "I hear you've been converted or something?"

I reminded him about that night at the party. He'd been so stoned that he remembered nothing of what he'd said or done. But I told him that it was because of that incident that I had begun my search for God.

"You're joking, Darby," he said, amazed.

"It's true," I told him. "As you said those words something clicked in me and I've never looked back since."

He was stunned.

"Come on," I said. "Let's go and have a coffee and talk about it."

This started a pattern of regular meetings where I would tell Paul about Jesus. A few years later Paul committed his life to Jesus when he attended a special evangelistic meeting. I was thrilled when he phoned to tell me.

I was beginning to feel that maybe, just maybe, the strong desire I had to tell others about Jesus was leading somewhere. I wasn't sure where exactly, but I wondered if God had a greater purpose for me. Once again it was Paul who got me thinking when, after a couple of hours in the café one day, he said,

"You're really full of this aren't you? *Have you ever thought of becoming a preacher, Darby?*"

8
DISCOVERING WHAT I WAS MADE FOR

We were running up and down the sports hall like idiots.

"Steve, over here, pass the ball!"

My friend Mike was waving his arms around. Being a bit overweight he was sweating and out of breath. Charging down the hall with the ball gave me an exhilarating feeling of freedom. The only sport I'd been involved in before was fighting at football matches, so this was a new experience for me; one I never thought I'd have due to my drug-centred lifestyle. I was pretty good at both football and rugby.

Mike kept shouting at me to give him the ball. I knew from experience that when he got it, his feet would go all over the place and the ball would not reach its intended destination. Nevertheless, I passed the ball to him and then heard a loud groan from the spectators. He'd done it again. I was still surprised to see how normally gentle Christians were transformed on the football pitch, becoming quite aggressive. Admittedly, I wasn't any better. A few times I'd come close to giving someone a good hiding in the heat of the moment. It was only the grace of God that had held me back!

After the match, however, whatever had happened on the pitch was forgotten and both sides would be good friends again. Sitting on the bench with his head in his hands, Mike would bemoan our fate when we lost – which thanks to him was often.

"Where did we go wrong?" he would say. "Why didn't God help us?"

He took it all very seriously. I used to laugh at him and say he obviously hadn't been praying hard enough.

"Next time we'll win," he would say. But we hardly ever did.

Mike and I were good friends. He wasn't what I called a "typical" Christian. He saw the funny side of most things and had a sharp wit. When he was in full swing he would have me in stitches as he reeled off joke after joke. He was a lot of fun.

After playing football or rugby with new friends, my old life seemed a world away. Being able to take physical exercise and breathe fresh air was wonderful. I was gaining some weight after being fairly emaciated, and I now took an interest in my personal hygiene and appearance – things that were new experiences in my adult life.

After a good game of sport, with the hot water of the shower cascading over me, memories of cranking up faded. I still bore some of the physical scars of my previous way of life – small abscesses and faint needle track lines on my arms. But God had performed a miraculous transformation within. His faithfulness was so clear. I'd never had to ask anyone to pray for healing, because Jesus had stepped in and performed a miracle when I gave my life to Him. I knew that He was in control and that I didn't have to worry about a thing.

Over the coming months the scabs and abscesses healed up and I gave God all the praise for this. As a result of my lifestyle I was still slightly anaemic, but that didn't stop me from doing all the things I wanted to do.

I had begun to enjoy reading. The last time I had actually read books was at school – and even then very rarely. I was too busy with my own agenda. Books, in my opinion, couldn't teach me what I wanted to know about life. But now, there was nothing I looked forward to more than making a cup of tea and sitting immersed in a book. My life had truly changed.

One of the pivotal books for me – as it was for many who became Christians around this time – was *Run Baby Run*, the conversion story of gang member Nicky Cruz. What most stood out about his story was that despite having had a similar lifestyle to me, which involved lying, stealing, drugs and prison, God still used him. God turned his life around so that he spent his time leading people to Christ on the streets of New York. What an encouragement! One of Nicky's converts was Sonny Arguinzoni, who went on the become the pastor of a large church. Sonny also founded the ministry Victory Outreach, to reach the outcasts and marginalised of society with God's love, hope, and practical help. This ministry has impacted thousands of lives.

I had a similar desire to lead people to Jesus, the Great Transformer of lives. He had lifted me out of a deep, dark pit where, humanly speaking I was beyond help. He had brought me into liberty with Him. I wanted to spend the rest of my life telling everyone I came into contact with about Him. It was the least I could do.

As I looked back over the past weeks and months, and considered all the things about me that had changed, it wasn't because my parents or other people had told me to change – it was all down to God. He was gently and gradually erasing the old me and building up the new. Even my taste in music had changed. Wishbone Ash, Yes and Bob Dylan had been my favourites and I would crank up to their familiar songs. But now when I tried to play that music the association with painful memories was just too strong, too raw. I decided to get rid of all those albums.

There weren't a lot of young people at our church, but I still enjoyed going there. I hated working on Sundays and always tried to request them off so that I could go and spend time with God's people. As time wore on, I began to realise that Christians are just like the rest of the human race – subject to small-mindedness and pettiness at times. I found that difficult to come to terms with initially, because I was still on cloud nine. But, I could see that it takes God a lifetime to remould us and form us into the image of Christ. This does not hinder Him from using us for His glory in the meantime.

As for girlfriends, at the moment I wasn't really interested. I wanted to keep my mind focused on Jesus and not be distracted. I briefly went out with one girl who seemed spiritually "on the ball", but we both came to the conclusion that we would be good friends and nothing more. I was never short of attention. As soon as I set foot in the church I would have a few girls coming to chat to me. But looking back, I have to admit that I was the only young man available, which is why I commanded so much attention!

My pastor, David Tinnion, helped me a great deal in my early days as I struggled to live out my newfound faith in Christ. He suggested that it would be good for me to get involved with the youth group. I felt I knew next to nothing about teenagers, but David believed in me enough to ask me, so I couldn't refuse. I became a youth leader and gained confidence in relating to young people, speaking publicly, and having to make wise decisions. Many of the youth came from nominally Christian backgrounds and some of them found it hard to live the Christian life due to the pressures they faced at home.

The youth group began to grow as these same young people invited their friends to the meetings. As I spent time with the teenagers, counselling them as they talked about their fears and worries, I could see the changes they were going through and this in turn had an effect on me. I had never really wanted to listen to other people's problems – especially not kids – because I was consumed with my own problems. But now I was advising and helping them.

The grim, day to day reality of life in Four Squares, Liverpool, was far removed from my life now. Back then, if someone had told me that by the age of twenty I would be happy and contented, living at home with my mum and dad, they wouldn't have got to the end of the sentence. But it was true: I was genuinely happy and content, supported by loving parents.

Looking back, it was extraordinary to me how I could have so misread their intentions towards me. Dad and I had regular Bible studies together and prayed together as often as we could. My sister Norma became the hard-hearted one. I tried sharing my faith with her, but she would immediately switch off and change the subject. I had thought that since she had seen first hand all I had been through – how, miraculously, I was still alive to tell the tale and how Jesus had changed me – this would be enough to convince her of the power of Christ. But I was wrong. She remained unreceptive. Our relationship was certainly a lot better than it had been, since she had left home and got married, but nothing I did or said swayed her. She wasn't interested.

Meanwhile, the reality of the deep needs of humanity hit me every time I walked through the doors of the hospital where I worked. I was on the Acute Admissions ward. All and sundry were admitted, from park bench down-and-outs to well-educated professionals. It seemed that no section of society was immune from mental illness; the ward was constantly packed. No sooner was a bed vacated than it was filled with someone else.

Many of the patients' behaviour was bizarre and aggressive. One young man suffered from epilepsy and spent most of the day in bed. The Charge Nurse, however, had decided that all patients needed to be motivated and that no one should remain in the dormitories during the day. This patient obviously hadn't heard about the new ruling, because when I encouraged him to get out he refused to move. I approached him tentatively, and moved to gently peel the bed sheet off him, but in an instant he sprang up and lashed out at me. I ducked just in time. He continued swinging for me, but I was helped by a fellow staff member.

Working on a busy psychiatric ward was like working on the frontline. On another occasion I was dealing with a man who used to sit in the day-room, never changing position for hours on end. Eager to get him moving, I approached him, but he wasn't having any of it. He sprung up out of his chair like a grizzly bear rearing up on its prey, lifted me off my feet and threw me against a wooden partition. I was still hanging onto him and we both crashed through it. Days later I was still picking splinters out of my skin.

Surely, I thought, *God must have something better for me than this? Something that doesn't involve strong-arming.* Besides me, there was only one other Christian in the hospital and some of the staff objected to me sharing Jesus with the patients.

Simon was the psychologist attached to our ward. He was an atheist who thought that anyone who believed in God deserved a bed on the ward. He was always questioning my beliefs and wasn't convinced that I had been transformed. His justification for this view was that my former life can't have been as bad as I was making out.

One afternoon, when things were quiet on the ward for a change, he invited me to join a group of colleagues to discuss my faith. I was happy to attend, taking any opportunity to share the good news of the gospel. Simon asked me to talk about my experience and as I talked about my life he and his colleagues made notes, looking at me in utter disbelief. After some time I sensed that I was getting nowhere with them. I recalled a conversation with an older Christian who had said that whenever you found yourself in such a situation, the thing to do was to get back to the Bible and explain why Jesus Christ had to die. So that's what I did.

I felt that Simon wanted to respond to what I had to say, but I also sensed he would only go so far in front of his colleagues. He soon called the meeting to an end. But God is gracious and allowed me to meet up with Simon one more time. He talked about his life and admitted that he didn't feel fulfilled. Shortly after this he was moved to another ward, but I prayed for him and hoped that one day he would surrender his life to Jesus.

Meanwhile, our evangelism efforts at the church were bearing fruit. Every week there seemed to be a few new faces. Our street outreach was successful and people were responding to the gospel. Unemployment in the area was up and despair was often written on people's faces. They needed answers to their troubled lives. Drugs and alcohol were menaces that were destroying lives and families. For such people, reaching out for Jesus was a much needed lifeline.

The church enjoyed a growing positive reputation and it wasn't long before BBC Radio Merseyside approached David and asked if they could record our Sunday service for one of their religious programmes. In a few weeks, the crew duly arrived with all their equipment, got set up, and the service got underway. We started off by singing some songs. Then the producer asked us to "speak in tongues". David tactfully explained that the gift of tongues wasn't meant to be used lightly. The next item was me giving my testimony. I only had to speak for three or four minutes, but I was still nervous.

The service finished and the radio crew packed up their stuff and left. I thought that was the end of that. When the programme was broadcast I listened to it with my parents and it came across well. But the result of my testimony being heard throughout the region was that other Elim churches invited me to come and speak to their congregations. Probation officers also wanted me to speak to their young offenders, and schools and colleges asked me to come and speak to their students. It was an exciting time for me and I found myself travelling to different parts of the country, meeting lots of new people, praying for and encouraging others. I felt that this was God's purpose for me.

But as time went on, the novelty of travelling so much wore off. I was tired of jumping on and off trains and smiling when sometimes I didn't feel like it. I also got annoyed that some Christians seemed to relish hearing the details of my former life a bit too much. In hindsight I was probably trying to be all things to all people and that was unsustainable. I had to admit that I wasn't bringing glory to the name of Jesus. I was the one who was getting all the praise: "You're doing really well, Steve … You're so brave … You've come such a long way in your faith…".

I would bask in the praise of others, but ultimately it didn't make me feel good. On the train home I would feel guilty that I was doing this for all the wrong reasons. As I stood on the platforms of various churches, people young and old would drink in all I had to say and I could see on their faces that they were completely caught up in my story. But all this was never supposed to be about me.

I didn't tell anyone what was going on inside me and for a while I lived a double life. By day I was happy and confident, fearless and willing to do anything to serve Jesus. By night I was a nervous wreck, bombarded with doubts and guilt; full of fear that God would repay me for my wrong motives.

Although God had miraculously transformed me, I was still

on a journey to maturity in Christ and there were still struggles. At times I suffered with horrendous nightmares and I was frightened to go to sleep. After my parents had turned in for the night, I would hang around in the living room, delaying going to bed for as long as possible. I knew that as soon as I fell asleep the nightmares would arrive.

They were so real that even to recall them is horrible. Most were dominated by the terrible fights I used to have. Images of distorted faces loomed forward, magnified, vividly capturing every detail. I lay in bed trying to stay awake, quietly singing choruses or praying, begging God not to let my sleep be troubled that night. Nothing seemed to work. The darkness would creep over me and rest heavily on my body. As I drifted into sleep, they would begin.

Sometimes I would see myself standing in an open space with an axe in my hand, then I would hear a motorbike in the distance. Slowly the rider would get closer and closer to me until it looked as though he was going to run me down. I would lift the axe and swing it, knocking the rider to the ground. Then a terrible battle would ensue. All the while I could hear nothing but terrible screaming and would wake sweating and breathless, my heart pounding. I was relieved that the experience hadn't really happened, but I was gripped in the stranglehold of fear, so that sleep became my enemy.

Sometimes I would be the onlooker in the nightmare. I would be outside of my body, watching myself have a heart attack. I would be strapped onto a trolley being wheeled into the A&E department, with a paramedic planting defibrillator pads onto my chest and shocking me. My whole body would convulse, lifting off the trolley and slamming back down. Then I would hear a doctor call out, "It's no use. He's dead. Let's move him out."

I would try to cry out, to tell the doctor that they must keep trying, but I was unable to move or speak. The frustration was unbearable. Then a nurse would pull a sheet over my head and I would be plunged into darkness. The weight of the sheet seemed suffocating and I began to gasp for breath as my body went into spasms.

No other person knew about the torment I was going through. Who could I tell? Not my parents. My dad would have wanted to set up camp in my room to watch over me. And I felt unable to tell my pastor because I didn't want him to think that I needed help. So I kept it to myself.

Whilst most of my nightmares were horrific fantasies, the nightmare that threatened to become a reality was the one in which I was enticed back onto drugs. I would find myself at a party surrounded by faceless people. A man would approach me with a needle and syringe. At first I would be strong and push him away. I was aggressive about it, angry that he was trying to seduce me back into my old ways. I shoved him or hit him. But he would come back again and again. Over time his persistence began to wear me down. In the end I would weakly submit to him and he would tie a tourniquet around my arm. Just as he pierced my skin with the tip of the needle, I would wake up in a cold sweat.

The thought of sliding back into my old ways was terrifying and abhorrent to me. Even though I knew that Jesus would enable me to overcome the temptation, I knew I would rather die than succumb to it. I prayed about it a lot and, as I continued to witness to my friends, I stayed on constant guard in case they offered me some gear or tried to slip something into my drink.

The fact that I wasn't sleeping was beginning to show on my face. I badly needed help and encouragement. One Sunday, at the evening service, an elderly lady walked in and during the meeting she prayed out loud – it was an incredible prayer, full of truths from the Bible and full of life. I felt so lifted up and encouraged by her words that I went to speak to her at the end of the service. We made arrangements to meet up to pray together.

Mrs Robinson was a frail but alert old lady who said that she had heard my testimony on the radio and was delighted to have the privilege of meeting me. In Mrs Robinson I had at last found someone with whom I could share all that had been happening to me: the nightmares, the fears, the guilt.

She was very clear and direct. She told me that I needed to grow and mature in my faith. She explained that there were no short cuts to this and that it would take time and effort to achieve. I was prepared to do anything to overcome my problems. I would discipline myself by spending at least 30 minutes each day, or as much time as I could, reading my Bible and praying. At first it was hard – there were always other things competing for my attention – but as time went on, I had a growing desire to meet with Jesus.

I didn't understand everything I read in the Bible and, admittedly, at first my prayers were simply a shopping list of requests. But gradually I felt a lightness in my spirit and it was a pleasure spending time with Jesus. It was a few weeks before I suddenly realised that the nightmares were becoming far less frequent. Before long they ceased altogether.

My reading material had changed from the daily tabloids to the classic book *The Normal Christian Life* by Watchman Nee. Up until then, I had thought that the Christian life revolved around going to church on Sunday, witnessing to a few other people, giving money and, most of all, just surviving the trials and tribulations of each day until Jesus returned or called me to Himself.

Watchman Nee, however, spoke about walking with God,

allowing Him to have access to every little part of my life, and spending time in prayer. Not just presenting God with my shopping list, but telling Him how much I loved Him and letting Him speak back to me. It would take some time for me to actually put this into practice.

At first when I prayed, thoughts would come into my mind like, "God isn't listening … you're wasting your time…" or "God won't pay any attention to you – you're useless!" It was difficult to clear my mind of such thoughts, especially when I half believed them myself. I felt that I didn't have any special talent for anything; I wasn't an eloquent public speaker; I couldn't play an instrument and I certainly couldn't sing. But I persisted and, bit by bit, began to get closer to God.

During my lunch breaks at Rainhill Hospital I would go for a walk in the grounds, read my Bible and talk to Jesus. After a while I could hardly wait for lunchtime, so that I could keep my appointment with God. It was during these lunchtime meetings that God spoke to me and began to reveal His will for my life. I felt that I wouldn't spend the rest of my life working at the hospital, but that God wanted to use me to help people who weren't Christians and encourage those who were. How all this would come about He didn't reveal to me at this point, I just became aware that Jesus was in charge and that He would make it happen in His time. I kept all of this to myself at first – perhaps because sometimes I felt that I might be imagining it all.

On one of my visits to Mrs Robinson, I plucked up the courage to tell her what I thought God had told me. She responded positively.

"Steve, as I have been praying for you, the Lord has said exactly the same thing to me. He is going to use you to bring people to Himself."

I was amazed.

"He told you about me?"

Smiling, she nodded.

"Now all you have to do is wait and He will gently guide you into all truth."

Inside I felt electrified with excitement. I wondered why Jesus would want to use me when I didn't deserve His favour. But I was beginning to realise how big and powerful God really is and how He uses ordinary people to bring about His purposes – despite all their flaws and failings.

God also used His word to confirm what He wanted me to do. In my daily reading of the Bible, the Holy Spirit illuminated certain passages to me. I read about Moses and how God had called him to represent His people before Pharaoh. Moses' reaction was to tell God he couldn't do it, because he wasn't equipped and didn't have the necessary talents to accomplish the task. But God had other plans.

Another friend from church approached me one weekend and told me that God had said very similar things about me. I was surprised and pleased that God was making things plain to me. Not long after this, a guest speaker at the church picked me out of the congregation and told me that God was going to use me. I felt a hot wave of embarrassment come over me as he spoke about God's intentions for me. But I wanted to do whatever Jesus wanted me to do. If He could tell strangers that He had specific plans for me, who was I to argue?

By this time my daily readings had progressed into Jeremiah and I read about God telling Jeremiah that even before he was born, He'd known him and had his whole life mapped out. The words came to me with great force and I knew the Holy Spirit was speaking them directly to me. I knew, without a shadow of a doubt, that my life would be spent serving the Lord in whatever capacity He chose.

Like anyone, I had my own ideas about what that might look like. My dream was to be a missionary anywhere where there was sun, sea and sand! I saw myself hopping on and off planes, jetting around the globe. Just being the boring old pastor of a church didn't grab me. Although I knew it was an option, I never thought about it for long.

In God's wisdom, however, He accomplishes some things miraculously in our lives, whilst He is content for other things to work themselves out over time as we mature in Christ. One of the things that was "working itself out" in my life was my language. Although it had improved dramatically, using foul language had been second nature to me – every other word was a swear word. I still struggled with it. For a start, my thoughts were punctuated with terrible words. Then, it was hard work containing myself when I was around other people, having a laugh, and my guard was down. Swear words threatened to come tumbling out of my mouth before I realised what I'd said.

One Sunday morning after church, for example, some dear old ladies and I got into conversation. I began telling them some story when the inevitable happened. At first I didn't realise that I'd said something awful, but the looks on their faces told me everything – their mouths hanging open in disbelief. I apologised quickly and walked away rapidly!

As I walked home that morning I felt ashamed, but as I began to pray about it and asked the Lord to forgive me, I also realised that maybe those ladies were somewhat intolerant and found it hard to appreciate that we are all on a journey.

Over time, my bad language subsided and I knew my swearing days were over. No longer did I have to guard my mouth. I could speak freely without the fear of something inappropriate slipping out.

In church one Sunday evening I spotted a face I recognised from my past. I couldn't quite place him at first and thought he might have been a friend from my old days. After the service I went over to speak to this guy and discovered that we had gone to school together. Brian told me that he had committed his life to Jesus and was now attending Birmingham Bible College.

Currently he was on vacation, so we spent quite a lot of time together that summer. Throughout our time Brian kept telling me how much he was enjoying Bible college and he asked me if I'd considered going. I laughed.

"Me? You must be joking! I was expelled from school. There's no way any college – let alone a Bible college – would have me."

"Bible college is different from other colleges," Brian said. "It's full of people whose lives have been changed by Christ. You would fit right in."

I said nothing. The truth was, deep down I would have loved to go to Bible college, but I just couldn't imagine how it could happen. Surely they wouldn't want *me*?

That summer Brian invited me to go to Liverpool with him. I asked him what he was doing and he told me he was visiting some friends who worked on a ship. The ship turned out to be the *Logos*, belonging to the ministry Operation Mobilisation. OM sent ships around the world distributing Christian literature and helping to meet people's needs.

I agreed to go and, arriving at Liverpool docks, I was amazed at the size of the ship – it was enormous. Brian and I were shown around and I was impressed with the amount of books and leaflets they had to give away, and by the commitment of the staff who served the ministry. Over lunch Brian and I chatted with a number of them and I began to feel that I'd like to work alongside them. Even the terrible ship's food didn't put me off! I asked someone,

"How would I go about applying to work on the *Logos*?"

"Well, you'd need your pastor's recommendation," they replied.

I thought that would be no problem. Maybe this was what God wanted for me? Talking it over with Brian later, he thought I might be right. I began to get all excited about it and I could already see myself sunbathing on deck or strolling down a golden beach somewhere!

I told Dad about it. He was pleased that I was keen to do something like this, but thought it might be a bit premature for me to thrust myself into frontline ministry.

"But Dad, I know I could do it," I insisted. I had my mind set on going on the ship and that was that. David, my pastor, brought me down to earth with a bump.

"I don't think you're ready to go," he told me straight.

"Why not?" I asked, shocked.

"Because you're not mature enough yet in your faith to handle all the responsibilities that would be put on you," he told me.

"But David, I know myself and I believe it's time," I protested.

Pausing for a moment, David looked at me and said gently, "Steve, come back to me in 12 month's time and we'll have another talk and see where things are at."

I was really deflated and despondent, my hopes and expectations of serving the Lord snatched away. Since becoming a Christian I had been on a high, overcoming many obstacles and continuing to walk with Jesus. The idea of a new chapter of my life opening up by joining the crew of the *Logos* seemed like the icing on the cake. I had felt that this was what I'd been building up to, but now the dream was over.

I started to question God about it. I wondered if He had, in fact, spoken to me, or if it was just a product of my imagination. Those people who had had prophetic words for me about the Lord using me – had they got it wrong too?

This was a critical time for me in my faith. I started to feel unsure of myself and began to analyse everything that was said to me, as well as everything I thought. As a result, my prayer life went downhill. Although I continued with my daily studies, I took on an unhelpful sense of condemnation, as though God was displeased with me because I had got things wrong. Of course, that wasn't true, but that was my perception of the situation. Mrs Robinson put me right. She could see that I was troubled and one day asked me what the problem was, so I told her.

"Steve, I must say that I feel David was right," she told me. "You have a lot of energy and enthusiasm for serving God, which is wonderful. But God is working in your heart right now and continuing to change you. When He has completed that work, then He will release you and you will be able to confidently work for Him."

With these words, the resentment I felt inside ebbed away and I felt a lot better. I understood that God was at work in me, and that in His time and way, He would release me into what He had prepared for me to do.

It was around this time that I became aware of people speaking about the baptism in the Holy Spirit. I had read about it in the Bible and wanted to experience it for myself. People chatted to me about their experience of receiving the Holy Spirit, and I was surprised that my experience didn't match theirs. I certainly hadn't had the same kind of experience and this upset me. I attended lots of meetings where people were prayed for to receive the Spirit's anointing, but somehow I didn't receive it. It seemed like the Lord didn't want me to have it, or so I thought. It would be a while before it happened to me.

Around this time David announced that BBC Radio Merseyside would be coming to the church again to record an evening service. He asked if I would like to give my testimony again and I said yes without hesitation. It was an exciting prospect to be on the radio again. I spoke again about my former life and how God had changed me, only this time I was far more composed and less nervous. I didn't rehearse a speech this time either, I just trusted God to speak through me.

Over the following weeks I began to receive phone calls from the leaders of various local churches who had heard the broadcast and wanted me to speak at their events. Here I was, going down the same road as before. Why wasn't God letting me do something different? But I still went along to the churches and spoke.

I was asked to speak at the church that I used to attend with my parents as a child. Nerves assailed me as past memories flashed through my mind. It seemed a lot smaller than I remembered and, as I was shown around the Sunday school rooms, I thought of all the times I had been thrown out for bad behaviour! In fact, that was how I was introduced that evening: "One of the most difficult Sunday school pupils this church has ever had"! Starting on that note, I rushed through what I had to say and within ten minutes I'd finished. I had wanted to speak for longer, but nervously I'd whizzed through it.

Later, however, as I mingled with the people, they said how pleased they were that I'd become a Christian and spoke lots of words of encouragement. A small minority had taken it personally when I'd said that as a kid I'd found the church incredibly boring!

After this, more invitations came in for me to travel around the country, and off I went again. The most exhilarating part for me was seeing people respond to the gospel message and come to Christ. I continually thanked God for dying for my sins – of which there were many – and for accepting me and using me to reach others.

But as before, it wasn't long before my busy speaking schedule had me feeling guilty about myself again. Physically, emotionally and spiritually I was drained. My Bible study was nearly non-existent and my prayer life was barren. Things began to get on top of me and even the simplest decisions were getting to be too much.

I found myself confiding once more in Mrs Robinson. She told me what no one else had.

"Stop travelling the country giving your testimony and give that time over to the Lord."

I felt disappointed, but relieved too. I realised that David and Mrs Robinson had both been right. My latest experience of ministry had proven that. At that time, I didn't have the spiritual maturity and stamina needed to sustain a busy ministry schedule. I knew that God wanted me to share my testimony with others – that was clearly the right thing to do – but not at the expense of intimacy with Jesus. Although I was going around seeking to encourage and build up others, I wasn't allowing the Lord to build me up.

Turning down invitations to speak was really hard at first, but I knew it was a choice between spending quality time with the Lord or doing my own thing. Thankfully, Jesus won. Settling back into the routine of church life wasn't difficult and I was soon caught up again in evangelism, back on the streets of St Helens.

Once a year, all the Elim churches met together for a week-long conference. That year it was held in a Butlin's holiday camp in Clacton-on-Sea. Just before I went I saw Mrs Robinson again. She told me that I would have a good time there.

"Yes, I'm looking forward to it," I told her.

"You never know, something special may happen to you that will change your life," she said cryptically.

"What?" I asked. I wondered if God had said something specific to her about me.

"Oh, I don't know," she said with a twinkle in her eye. "You never know with God. Just be prepared."

9
A LIFE TRANSFORMED

A group of coaches were parked side by side in the Keele service station, the first stop on the way from St Helens to Clacton-on-Sea. I heard someone call out my name:

"Hey, Darby!"

I looked around and didn't spot who was calling.

"Over here!"

It was Keith, an old friend of mine I'd not seen since I'd left school. He looked exactly the same as he'd always done, just bigger.

"Hey, how are you?" I was surprised and pleased to see him.

"What are you doing here, miles from home?" he asked.

I noticed that he was wearing the colours of the Saints, St Helens rugby team. He and hundreds of other supporters were travelling to Wembley to see them play. I was a bit envious. I would have loved to go too.

"I'm on my way to Clacton," I told him, mumbling slightly.

"What's that? I didn't hear you."

Just then an old lady from another church came up and asked me where the toilets were. I pointed her in the right direction and blushed in embarrassment when Keith said,

"Who's that, your granny?"

I explained that I was on my way to the coast for a church week away.

"Have you lost the plot or what?" he said. "What's all this

business with the church?"

I told him of my recent experiences and how I had become a Christian. He didn't appear to be very interested. He only had the rugby on his mind.

"I can't get my head around how you're going to Clacton and not Wembley, Darby," he said.

I knew where he was coming from, but the pull to be with God's people, worshipping Him, was stronger. He had changed me a great deal.

* * *

The holiday camp was packed with around 5,000 people, the vast majority of whom were Christians. I was amazed to see so many young, trendy people who were Christians. This certainly wasn't going to be a boring week.

One of the first young people's meetings I attended was a gathering of several hundred, all eager to praise God loudly and enthusiastically. The air was buzzing with excitement. The speaker for this session was a Canadian called Danny Moe. Just hearing Danny speak about Jesus revolutionised my life. He was a good musician and had set lots of Scripture to song. He got us all praising God and dancing around. As we repeated the words of the choruses over and over, truth seeped into me and I left the meeting on a massive high.

During the meeting people around me had been praying and singing in tongues and I longed to be able to do this myself. Not a day went by when I didn't pray and ask God for this gift. I knew that the gift of tongues came as a result of being baptised in the Holy Spirit, and that it would enrich my prayer times and strengthen every area of my life. I needed the empowering of the Spirit in order to do the things that Jesus had in store for me.

While I was at Clacton I attended some "waiting meetings", which were just what they sound like: meetings in which people would wait before God for the Holy Spirit to come and touch those who were prayed for. I found them quite frightening. I waited with a group of others for ministers to lay hands on us and pray for us. The atmosphere was quite intimidating. The men doing the praying would pray loudly in tongues, then clamp their hands on each person, practically shaking and squeezing them, as though they were trying to beat the Holy Spirit into them. After each such meeting I came out in a daze, wondering what had hit me. But for all the theatrics, I never received the baptism of the Holy Spirit.

Towards the end of the week, my determination not to go home the same as I had come had mounted, and one morning I got up very early to spend time with the Lord. Again I asked Him to baptise me with His Spirit. I could sense God's presence in the room, closer to me than before. I lay face down on the floor and began to worship Jesus. As I did, my skin began to tingle and a warmth grew inside me. I began to shake. Throughout this experience I was unable to utter a word – it was a moment too holy for words. I just lay there and drank in the awesome presence of God.

After several minutes, words began to form deep within me. It wasn't my normal mode of speech. Before I knew what was happening, words began to burst out of my mouth. I didn't stop to analyse it, I just said the words. I knew that they were words of blessing and praise to God. I don't know how long I was like this, but gradually my mind began to take over and I was able to think about what had taken place. I knew that I had finally received what I wanted from the Lord. I could see why He had withheld it from me until now. He wanted me to be completely alone with Him, so that He could speak to me without the interference of others, and so that I would know without a shadow of a doubt that it was genuine.

The sense of the close presence of God subsided a little, but for the rest of the day His peace was with me. I knew I was a changed person. From that moment on I felt a new boldness to tell people about Jesus. At lunch, as the waiters moved around the room, I felt an urge to speak to the waiter at our table. I asked him about himself and what it was like working at the holiday camp. Then I told him briefly about my experience of working in a camp in north Wales, and then about the difference Jesus had made in my life. He was very polite, but the conversation didn't go any further. I didn't mind – I prayed and committed him to God. I was thankful for this new confidence. It enabled me to overcome any hesitance to speak the truth with grace, regardless of how I was feeling. I felt empowered by the Holy Spirit and I knew that God was further preparing me for His future plans. At the first meeting I attended after my experience of the Holy Spirit I was able to pray and praise in tongues. In fact, I couldn't stop. It was like a tap that couldn't be turned off.

The group of young people from my church spent most of our time together. When there weren't any youth meetings we were always in the café. We got friendly with lively groups of youth from Guernsey and Northern Ireland. Sometimes we spent the whole evening in the café chatting until it closed. We would talk about the things God had done and was doing in our lives. When I shared my testimony everyone praised God that He had brought me through such a hard time and I was now able to tell others about His mercy and forgiveness. There were about twenty of us in all, full of joy and keen to get out there and serve God.

Two of the girls in our group came from Guernsey. They really stood out (as far as I was concerned) and I spent a lot of my time chatting to them. But one of the girls in particular, Julia Migasiuk, was a real live wire. She was constantly talking about Jesus in a refreshing and vibrant way. I was really encouraged by being in her company. By the end of the week I was very happy that I'd come and had no regrets whatsoever on missing out on a mundane game of rugby.

All too quickly the week was over and we were loading our bags back onto the coach. Parting from our new friends was a bit sad, but we all exchanged phone numbers and addresses, making promises to keep in touch. I made sure I got Julia's number!

Travelling home I reflected on the past week and thanked God for all He was doing in my life; for the total turnaround He had accomplished. Julia had commented on my appearance. It was true that I was still thin and ill-looking, but I was suffering from anaemia and my blood system was only slowly getting back into order. My hair was also rather long. All this was superficial though – my heart and mind had been radically changed, and my spirit brought to life in Christ. Fundamentally, I was a new person.

I couldn't wait to get to church on Sunday. Now that I could speak in tongues I just wanted to praise God. During the worship time I lifted my hands up high and began to praise God at the top of my voice – just like I'd been doing all week in Clacton. I was completely oblivious to everyone around me. After the service, David took me to one side and told me that in future he would appreciate it if I kept the noise down. I ought to consider the needs of others and not be a nuisance!

I felt wounded. In my unbounded enthusiasm it was difficult to understand his reasoning. I had been deeply touched by God and I just wanted others to be drawn into that experience too. What could be wrong with that? When I prayed about it later, I felt it would be best just to conform to what David wanted. A few years later the whole church became caught up in the same excitement in praising God.

Until now, marriage was something that had rarely crossed my mind. If I did think about it, I quickly pushed it to one side. Close relationships seemed to demand too much. Plus, I had never met anyone with whom I really wanted to spend the rest of my life. Added to this was a layer of guilt and self-recrimination. I hadn't yet come to understand the fullness of the grace of God towards me – His sheer, unmerited favour. I assumed that God wouldn't give me a good-looking girl who had all the qualities a man could wish for in a wife. I thought He would give me a grumpy, boring woman whose role in life was to keep me on the straight and narrow!

I looked at the scrap of paper on which Julia had scribbled her phone number and sensed that one day she would be my wife. I had not a scrap of evidence for such a thought, but somehow God seemed to sow this thought into my mind. Rationally speaking, Julia and I weren't at all suited to one another. She came from a middle-class background, and I from a working-class one. Julia's dad owned a hotel in Guernsey with a swimming pool. I lived in a terraced house with a tiny garden. I couldn't see her living in St Helens with its grey rows of little houses. The affluent residents of Guernsey would have shuddered at the likes of me and my drug-crazed friends. The more I thought about it, the more I wondered how this woman could ever, for one moment, consider being my wife.

Yet God gently persisted, allowing the thought to linger, and a few weeks on from the Clacton Bible week I called her. We chatted for a short while and I thought that was that. She didn't sound particularly interested in me and I thought, *I must have got it wrong.* I decided to leave the matter in God's hands. "Lord, if this is from you, please make a way for us to get together," I prayed.

Little did I know that God was at work in Julia's heart too and throughout this time she was thinking along the same lines. She had been praying about her future partner. She had once attended a youth conference in Belgium where Luis Palau was the main speaker. During one meeting he said that God was challenging everyone to put Him first in their lives. If God called you to be single, he said, would He still be first in your life? If you wanted to be married, would He still have pre-eminence? Luis went on to say that if you wanted to be married, you should start praying for your partner now, especially if the person wasn't yet saved.

Those words made a great impression on Julia and she began to pray for her husband to become a Christian. She felt God guide her specifically in this way. This happened right around the time I became a Christian.

A few months after I'd met Julia, her friend, Wendy, who went to my church told me that Julia would be coming to stay for a short while and would I mind picking her up from the airport? I didn't need to think about it – of course I said yes.

The day that Julia walked out through customs at the airport my stomach was doing somersaults. She looked absolutely radiant. She was tanned, her eyes sparkled, and she was easily the best dressed woman in the arrivals lounge! Silently, I prayed that I had heard correctly from God – that this lady would become my wife – though I still couldn't get my head around how it could all come about.

By the Wednesday of that week, however, I knew we would be together. We had spent a lot of time together and, as we talked, sharing our respective hopes and dreams, it seemed increasingly right for us to be together. During a day trip to north Wales, sitting on the banks of the river in Betwys-y-Coed, there was a sense of openness between us. To the sound of the gently flowing water I proposed and she accepted. It was as simple as that.

I marvelled at the goodness of God, praising Him as He guided my life in the way He wanted it to go. All that was required of me was to be obedient, willing to allow Him to do what He wanted to do. I just wanted to remain in the centre of His will.

Julia felt that the Lord was calling her to work in St Helens and take an active part in the church, so in October 1976 we got engaged. I was dreading meeting Julia's parents for the first time, since Julia had told them all about my past life. But they never once condemned me for my past or tried to prevent me from marrying their daughter. They weren't Christians at the time, but God touched their hearts so that they accepted me without prejudice.

The following year we were married. I was still working at Rainhill Hospital and Julia was taking a crash course in secretarial skills. We were both heavily involved in the activities of the church. Julia had been elected to be on the Youth Committee and planned lots of different events. I remained part of the evangelism team and continued to work among the drug addicts of the town.

Our first year of marriage was hard. We both continued to seek the Lord regarding where He wanted us to be and what He wanted us to do. He answered very clearly – and it was the very thing I didn't want to hear! It would be serving Him as a pastor in the ministry. I wrestled with the thought of training to become a pastor. Memories of my past, mixed with feelings of guilt and unworthiness, besieged my mind. It was hard to push them out. Mistakenly, I thought that in order to be a pastor you had to have an unblemished background, which certainly ruled me out; besides which, I still felt that I was below par in terms of my education.

Julia was a tower of strength during this time. As we read God's word and prayed together I gradually overcame all my negative thoughts and resolved to be strong and serve God as a pastor if that's what He wanted me to do. I got excited by the prospect of maybe going to Bible college. We thought that we'd better go and talk this over with our pastor, David. He had other ideas.

"I don't think you need to go to Bible college," he said. "You can learn far more in the local church than you can in any Bible establishment. It's the practical experience you need, rather than the theory. I'll give you all the help you need."

"But David," I said, "we both feel this is not just something we want to do – we believe God's leading us in this direction."

We talked further and hoped that he could see this was God's doing, not ours. It took a while to convince him, but eventually he agreed to let us go.

* * *

The Elim Bible College was not how I imagined it would be. Most of the students were from the south of England and a lot of their families were already Christians. I stuck out like a sore thumb. I was a northerner with a background of drug abuse. I could scarcely be more different. For much of the time I carried around a sense of inferiority, because there was literally no one else of a similar background to mine at the college. Everyone seemed to come from a healthy Christian background and, annoyingly, they all seemed to be able to play the guitar!

However, after a while the barriers began to come down and I was able to mix with the other students. Our mutual love for the Lord overcame our differences and bound us together.

The study itself was hard going as we got to grips with biblical truth and Church history. I'm not stupid, but I had been expelled from school, so my literacy wasn't all it should have been and I had some catching up to do. Plus, I knew next to nothing about the context of the Bible. But I wasn't the only person who struggled.

Part of the coursework required me to deliver a sermon in front of the whole college, after which my tutors would critique what I'd said and criticise/praise it accordingly. All of us students knew this day was coming at some point. Personally, I was terrified about it. All my doubts and feelings of inferiority came rushing to the surface again. Who was I to stand up there and deliver a sermon in front of all these very experienced people?

As the time approached I was a babbling wreck. I had been praying for weeks that God might allow His Holy Spirit to use me when I spoke. The day finally came and I stood up in front of the whole faculty and the other students and began to deliver my message. I spoke about Jonah, painfully aware of my own nervousness and discomfort. I mumbled through my introduction and then gathered a little more courage to continue with what I had to say.

That day God answered my prayers in a spectacular way. It certainly wasn't the best sermon you will ever hear, but God in His grace turned up. An incredible, tangible sense of His presence filled the hall. It was all God's doing, but such was the powerful sense of His presence that everyone in the room was on their faces, repenting before Him.

Later my tutors said that because the Holy Spirit had moved amongst them, they couldn't really take issue with my message – it would have been like criticising the Spirit. Christopher Smith, the lead lecturer, commented,

"Steve has made loads of mistakes this morning, but we can't touch this!"

This had never happened before when I had preached. It was like receiving God's seal of approval on my ministry, which was hugely encouraging. I was elated and so thankful that God was with me. Even though I was a reluctant servant at times and found things difficult, the Lord proved time and again that He would see me through.

10
LEARNING THE ROPES

I had made it – I'd graduated from Bible college. Just a few years previously, such a thing would have been unthinkable. I was learning more and more about the nature of God – that if we try to put limits on what He can do, we will become disillusioned and stunted in our spiritual lives. We must be transparent and open before Him, and above all trust Him. God knows more about us than we know about ourselves, and His main desire is to grow and shape us into the person of faith He has planned for us to be.

After Bible College, and now an accredited minister with the Elim movement of churches, the next step was for me to be assigned to a church as an associate minister. The accepted way of doing things in the movement was for newly qualified ministers to be sent to churches other than their home church. I was offered a couple of churches towards the end of my time, but Julia and I didn't feel they were where God wanted us.

On one occasion I went to visit a church in Bootle, Merseyside, accompanied by my pastor, David Tinnion. It is no reflection on the church, but I just knew that this wasn't the place where I could thrive and be my best. On the way back, however, David told me that he really wanted me to come back to St Helens and join his staff full time, as his associate pastor. In my heart of hearts I wanted this too. It was the church where I'd been saved, pastored and mentored by David, and where everyone knew my background and understood where I was coming from. We both knew, though, that this was against the rules.

David approached the General Superintendent of Elim at the time, John Smith, and put the case to him. Initially he received a flat no in response: "Sorry, that's not the way we operate…". But David got into a debate with him and eventually John said that he'd like to speak to me. Eventually, I received a phone call from him. John is a great man, a terrific friend to this day, and someone who was and is a great support. We often laugh about the conversation we had.

John was the head of the Elim movement and I was a young, twenty-something upstart who must have appeared incredibly arrogant. John kept saying to me, "I don't feel this is right, Steve." I kept saying in response, "I need more than you not feeling this isn't right!" I explained that there was a group of elders in St Helens who wanted me to come and minister, and I believed God had more for me to do in this church. Eventually, John relented, but not without adding ominously,

"I'm going to allow you to do this, but this is a black mark on your record!"

Black mark or not, in time the ministry partnership between David and I would prove to be a great success.

* * *

Leaving the relative safety of Bible college and taking up your first role as an actual minister is a daunting challenge. When you are standing in front of a group of people who are looking to you for spiritual input and guidance, you become keenly aware of your responsibility, and of the stakes involved in getting it right or wrong. I knew that this was absolutely where God wanted me, but coming back to St Helens was perhaps harder because I would be leading those people who had helped me come to Christ, and who had mentored me through all my ups and downs. Perhaps this was part of the reasoning behind Elim's policy.

Julia and I also had the first addition to our family. Jemma was six months old by the time I graduated from Bible college. Coming back to St Helens was therefore made more challenging by the fact that we didn't have a house and needed somewhere to live. David put it to the church that we needed some accommodation until we could find a place of our own.

It was a fairly big ask to take on a couple with a very young child, but during these early days one couple in the church, Ken and Beryl Barton, were amazing to us and welcomed us into their home. Ken and Beryl had recently lost a child at full term through stillbirth. Julia and I were sensitive to the fact that we had Jemma, and wondered how they would feel about that. We certainly didn't want to cause them any distress, but Ken and Beryl were just extraordinary.

Ken and Beryl set a great example for us of sacrificial service and hospitality. They also taught us so much about dealing with disappointment – facing the sometimes harsh reality of life without wavering in faith; without losing trust in God's goodness. They never spoke of their loss and they loved Jemma and made a great fuss of her.

We lived with them for about a year. During this time we were offered a number of different council accommodations, but Ken and Beryl were very protective of us. Ken looked at one place and was adamant, "There's no way you're moving into that!" They were happy to continue hosting us until we found exactly the right place. Our time with them was wonderful. They were just ordinary, down to earth people who loved the Lord.

Prior to Bible college, I had gradually become accustomed to standing at the front of the church to give a short word of encouragement. That was no problem. But now I was officially a pastor. Things were different! I would spend all week working on a sermon, changing it, adding to it, and by Sunday I was so nervous that I was almost physically sick before I preached.

My first sermon at the church was terrible. Just like the first time I'd shared my testimony in public, I wanted to run home and go into hiding as soon as the service ended. Yet, someone committed their life to Jesus at the end. Once again I was reminded that as long as I spoke God's word in truth, the delivery – good, bad or indifferent – was no obstacle to Him moving. He could still work in people's lives despite me.

Working alongside David Tinnion was a great experience for me. He was a great mentor. David never micromanaged me, preferring to allow me to take lots of risks in ministry and letting me learn from my own mistakes and successes. Ultimately, I think it came down to the fact that he didn't feel at all threatened by me. He was secure in himself and in his position. That meant he could give me the freedom to be myself.

As a result, I never felt any sense of frustration under David's leadership – something which is quite common among younger associate leaders who are maturing in ministry. David gave me space to develop and I never felt that he was holding me back or restricting me in any way. Rather, he was cheering me on. He recognised that my primary gifts were evangelism and leadership, and so he gave me opportunities to develop both.

David set a good example for me as senior leader, and I have since been able to transport those lessons into my own senior leadership, freeing up others to do what they do best without feeling insecure.

Meanwhile, I increased my work amongst the addicts of the town. Many of my friends had succumbed to the drugs and died, and as younger faces appeared to replace them, I was all the more driven to help them. I felt a great compassion for drug addicts and would go into the areas where they hung out in order to reach them.

In time, David took on the role of Regional Superintendent for our area, which meant that I carried much of the responsibility for the day to day running of the church. It was changing and growing. When I returned from Bible college we had around 100 members, but the church grew to 350 or so. The building we were in was nowhere big enough to accommodate that many people, so we knew we needed to find an alternative or build something from scratch. In the end, the latter was the best option, so in 1984 we began an ambitious project under God's guidance to build a new church complex. It was a big step of faith and required us to trust God deeply.

David managed this project whilst I ran the church and observed what he was doing, assisting him wherever I could. It was a fascinating learning curve and I discovered the many aspects of a project like this that need to be addressed. It was also an education to see how David, skilfully and purposefully, led and envisioned people in the church through this adventure. For instance, right in the middle of the build, the country was plunged into a recession and our area was hit harder than many. Lots of people were losing their jobs, which meant that the level of giving in the church suddenly dropped off. It left us with some financial challenges for a time, but David never lost sight of the bigger picture. We trusted God to help us navigate through this difficult time, and He did. Little did I know that all this learning would stand me in good stead for what I would need to do myself in the future.

Shortly after the new building was opened we held a service

at which I preached. I made an appeal for those who wanted to receive Jesus to come forward. I couldn't believe my eyes when I saw my sister, Norma, respond. Afterwards I went over to her and she told me, "You made it sound easy."

"It is!" I replied, overjoyed. Today Norma is a strong Christian and a vital part of her church.

Looking back, I think David and I worked so well together because we were both just so passionate about the local church being all that it could and should be. When I was at Bible college I used to read *Restoration* magazine, which at the time was *the* source of news about what was happening on the cutting edge of Pentecostal/Charismatic Christianity. What I read fired my imagination and excited me about what church could and should be. But then, at weekends us Bible students would be sent out into other churches in the vicinity of the college, and I would be disappointed by the reality I found. It was much different to what I was reading. I remember thinking, *Surely there must be more than this?*

The teaching that I read in *Restoration* – from the likes of Bryn Jones, Terry Virgo, Gerald Coates and others – revolutionised my thinking about church. Until we began working together, I didn't realise that David Tinnion was thinking along the same lines and was also reading and being inspired by *Restoration*. We shared the same vision to build a dynamic church that was effective in extending God's kingdom. That still sums up my vision today.

All in all, we were so happy in St Helens – which is why what happened next was a surprise.

11

CALLED TO SERVE

It was 1992 and we were well settled in St Helens. As I'd grown in experience and maturity, both as a believer and a leader, David had allowed me to take on more responsibility. He was wise enough to let me learn on the job and I had his reassurance that if I made a mistake, it wasn't the end of the world. As a result, we enjoyed great success and the church flourished.

The church had moved into its new building, the people were excited about it, and the church was buzzing. By this time there had also been two more additions to our expanding family! First Sophie and then Luke. We felt our family was complete and we were very happy.

It came as something of a surprise, then, when I began to feel unsettled in my spirit. Julia and I were content in the church – we had loads of good friends and the ministry was fruitful and fulfilling. We had no reason to leave the place that we loved. But deep down I began to feel the Holy Spirit gently tugging us away.

Other church leaders will testify to the fact that it's not unusual to feel "unsettled" in ministry. Alongside the excitement of following the Holy Spirit's lead and seeing God at work in situations, leaders have to do many things that are essentially "a job" – like admin, planning, having meetings about finance, etc. Sometimes people just feel like a change of scenery. But we need to analyse these feelings of unsettlement and discover whether it's

OUT OF THE RUINS

just "me" – my emotions – or something deeper. This time I knew that there was something more.

I also knew enough to know that it's not healthy to live out of a place of frustration and longing for something – whatever that something is. So I began to pray. At first I didn't mention to Julia how I was feeling. I didn't mention it to anyone, I just began a dialogue with God about whether He was trying to tell me something. I could see that if I simply came out and said, "I think God might be saying it's time for us to move on to something new," this would mystify Julia, and certainly David and the church. It was all going so well!

Around this time we attended the Elim churches annual conference. Whilst there, Phil Weaver, who at the time was the Regional Superintendent for Elim's London churches, approached me and said,

"You'll think that I'm crazy, Steve, but I'm going to ask you a question. Would you consider going to lead a church in Ilford?"

As far as Phil knew, I was completely settled and established in St Helens and probably there for life. That's why he felt unsure about mentioning it to me. Yet, he'd felt the Lord nudge him to do so.

As soon as Phil mentioned Ilford I felt my heart leap. Straight away my mind went back to my time in Bible college. I had been based in Dorking, Surrey, and I was assigned, every Sunday, to go to a church in East Ham. I drove up there and, en route, always dropped off a fellow student who had to get to Ilford but didn't have a car. I knew nothing about Ilford at all, but I recalled thinking, "There's something about this place!"

We'd also had the singer Helen Shapiro at our church recently to give a concert and oddly, during her talk, she had mentioned a particular shop that she used to go to in Ilford, which was known for its large Jewish community. Again, my heart leapt within me as the Holy Spirit sought to get my attention.

Without further hesitation I looked at Phil and simply said, "Yes, I'd be willing to go to Ilford."

After this, however, I needed to go and talk everything over with Julia!

I told her that I was pretty certain that God was calling us to a new season of ministry in a new town – and that place was Ilford. It was hard for her to hear. She was completely settled and happy in St Helens, so initially she just cried. But we agreed that we would pray about it together and see what God had to say.

I also went to see David Tinnion. It was premature to say that we were definitely leaving, but I also wanted to be completely transparent with him – to let him know that we were praying and seeking God about the future, and that it was likely He was calling us to a new place. David took the news well, but not without some disappointment. As his associate, David had high ambitions for me. He perhaps saw me one day taking over as senior minister. I truly appreciated all the love and support he'd given me over many years, but at the same time, I felt God's call to head south.

As part of the process Phil Weaver invited me to go down to Ilford to have a look at the church. I turned up there one Sunday morning, incognito. The church elders knew that I was visiting, but no one else. I was just a new face, popping in for a visit. That said, I certainly couldn't be missed because I was the only white person in the building! At that time, the church was predominantly a Ghanaian community.

I have to be honest and say that the church, as I found it, was not in great shape. When I returned home to St Helens Julia had lots of questions and wanted to know, "Is there anything good about the church?" – obviously looking to focus on some redeeming features. Hoping perhaps that I'd say, "It's got a fantastic community ministry" or "the kid's work is outstanding" etc., instead, I said,

"No, not really."

It wasn't what she wanted to hear.

Let me clarify that statement: I'm not saying that the church wasn't filled with lots of genuine, authentic Christians, because there were many. I didn't question the sincerity of people's hearts, just the expression of that faith. As a church it was lacking in so many different areas and suffered from being stuck in the past. It was bogged down with traditions that, as far as I could see, had little to do with vibrant faith and a meaningful expression of God's love. On top of that, the church building was run down, the worship was awful, and all the church elders were seated on the platform facing the congregation. Everything that I didn't like about church, I saw that day!

Despite all this, I told Julia,

"I really believe God wants us to go there."

In addition I explained to Julia that I didn't think I'd ever feel like I had really functioned in the call of God for my life, unless I went to Ilford and led the church under His guidance. One of the things I'd learned in my time in ministry was that a leader always has to see the bigger picture; the greater plan that God is unfolding. It's easy to get distracted by and bogged down in the details of the day-to-day, but we mustn't lose sight of the bigger thing God is doing, otherwise not only will we lose our heart and passion, we'll lose our way.

It would have been easy to focus on everything that was wrong with the Ilford scenario – all the negatives, all the things that needed to change, many of which would not be easy changes – but in my heart God had convinced me of the fact that He wanted to build a great church there, and I wanted to be part of that adventure.

Julia and I prayed about it more and we went to see David and the church elders in St Helens. I told them that I believed God was in fact calling us to Ilford, and that this was God's initiative; it wasn't just because Phil Weaver had invited me and I'd been down to visit the church. God was about something bigger and this was part of a process He'd been leading us through.

As my friend David Shearman is fond of saying, "If you belong, you can't leave, and if you don't belong, then you can't stay." I just knew that God had called Julia and me, and we couldn't stay any longer. To do so, out of comfort or even loyalty, would have been to settle for less than His best and, in the end, would have been counterproductive.

"I have loved every moment of serving the church here," I told the elders, "but I know that this time has come to an end."

* * *

Around this time there was a programme on TV about assistant leaders in churches. It featured a number of curates from Anglican churches, but amazingly also featured the very church we'd be going to in Ilford – known as City Gates church. I gathered Julia and the kids to sit down and watch the programme together. By this time our eldest, Jemma, was about to enter senior school; Sophie had just turned 6 and Luke was just 3 years old.

My predecessor in Ilford was Barry Killock and he had an associate leader called Glen serving alongside him. Glen would become my associate for the first seven months of my time as leader there. The church met in a small building on Clement's Road. When it was built in the 1960s it had been fairly progressive, but that was 30 years ago and nothing had moved on. It was a small, very traditional, church, surviving in a one-room building. It's fair to say that, compared to St Helens, it looked awful. By the end of the programme Julia, and all the kids, were crying. "*This* is where we're going?"

It was especially hard on Jemma, being older, and having an established circle of friends. She would be moving away from them, as she saw it, to the other end of the country. It might as well have been the other side of the world. It was difficult. I understood the emotions she was going through. Through this time we encouraged her to seek the Lord and find His reassurance for herself in the midst of this big change. As I reflect on these events now, it's encouraging to be able to write that Jemma did just that. She embraced the change and never looked back. God is so faithful and mindful of our needs. In due course, Jemma, Sophie and Luke, and of course, Julia, would all flourish in our new setting.

12
A NEW CHAPTER BEGINS

The first time Julia set foot in City Gates was at our induction service. As the service progressed I could literally see her sinking in her seat. The worship was a major contributor to her dismay. It was so different to what we were used to in St Helens. Later she told me that it felt like going back in time about 50 years. The old chorus, *I Keep Falling in Love With Him (over and over and over again)* was one that Julia was not fond of, to understate the matter. That day, they sang that chorus "over and over again" *ad nauseam*!

So many friends had come down from St Helens to attend the induction that they'd had to hire a couple of coaches for the trip. The place was packed. But I could see on their faces that they felt sorry for us. Our friends, who we'd spent so much of our lives with, were thinking, "Oh no, what have Steve and Julia come to?" And after the service had finished and all the goodbyes had been said, we had to return to our house – the church manse – alone. It was a bittersweet experience.

That night, as Julia and I lay in bed, newly inducted and on the brink of "day 1" in this new role, in a new town, far from all we had known, we experienced a terrible spiritual battle, the like of which we'd never known before. It was as though a thick, spiritual darkness descended and threatened to swallow us up.

Here we were, at this church in East London, that could

not have been any more different from what we had known; a church we knew very little about. We were well and truly out of our comfort zone. In fact, it was only later that I discovered four other people had been offered the leadership of this church and had turned it down!

I tossed and turned all night and was plagued with negative thoughts.

I have just gone and ruined everything for my family, I thought. It suddenly hit me that I had made a colossal mistake.

Although we didn't speak, I knew that Julia was awake, probably thinking the same thing. She knew that I was awake too, but we lay there in silence as the negative thoughts continued to crash in. I was thinking, *Tomorrow I'm going to have to contact Phil, apologise, and tell him that I have made a terrible mistake. Then I'm going to have to ask David if we can go back to St Helens.*

In the midst of this turmoil, Julia suddenly spoke.

"I know you're awake, Steve."

Then she delivered the word of the Lord, from Numbers 13. It was the phrase that was used by the fearful scouts who came to Moses, overwhelmed by the challenges of taking on the promised land.

"We have become like grasshoppers in our own sight, Steve," Julia said, "but God has called us here to do something."

As soon as she spoke these words, the cloud of spiritual darkness hanging over us left and light flooded in. At that moment, though I was certain there would be many challenges ahead, I knew for sure that we were in the place where God had called us. He was with us. We hadn't made a mistake; we had not been abandoned. Our lives were in His hands.

* * *

As I mentioned earlier, City Gates was essentially home to a

Ghanaian Christian community, made up of people who had emigrated to the UK. Historically, the Elim movement had sent missionaries to Ghana to preach the gospel and plant churches and a great Christian community had been established there. But, of course, many had decided to leave their own nation and move to England. Although connected to Elim for the time being, it was always the plan that the Ghanaian community would eventually find its own building to call home.

When I arrived as their new pastor I had to adjust rapidly to a very different culture to that which I'd known – which was easier said than done. To begin with, my leadership style was completely different to that of my predecessor. The way that I preached, the way that I ministered, were fundamentally different – a product of the way I had been discipled and mentored by David. Neither style was right or wrong – it was just that we were poles apart.

David Tinnion had taught me well as a young leader. One of the great pieces of wisdom he imparted to me was, "A new church is a weak church". As a new pastor in a new town, what I had was effectively a "new" church, despite all its history, so David advised me,

"Handle it like a new church. Don't think it's strong. There will be weaknesses that you have to address. As long as you are aware of that, you'll be fine."

Not assuming that the church was "strong" was helpful to keep in mind. It meant I needed to allow time to pass before introducing certain changes. It meant not releasing anyone into a full time position who wasn't really ready for it.

David had also taught me that it was helpful to have trusted friends to consult – experienced men of God who had lived through a great deal of church growth over many years – and who were outside of the church context; people who I could call upon to discuss any issue.

People like Alan Vincent, Wynne Lewis and Bob Gordon were always a listening ear through my early days in Ilford and a few tough times. Bob always had the ability to nail me if he thought I was out of order. I would be moaning to him about this and that issue and he, in his deep Scottish brogue, would cut across me and say,

"Son, what you're saying is correct, but your attitude needs to change!"

I didn't like hearing it at the time, but he was dead right. I'm very grateful for his loving correction now.

Alan Vincent has a prophetic edge and often brought the word of the Lord into my situation at just the right time. Wynne Lewis was very down to earth and a huge encourager of faith. He always pushed me to stretch myself beyond what I had believed God for in the past.

When a new minister arrives to take over the running of a church, not everyone is going to like you. It's just a fact. By nature, people like to be settled and we are all, to one degree or another, resistant to change. There are a minority who love, even thrive on change. But most people embrace it reluctantly!

As much as you would like to fit in as a leader, the fact is, you just can't. You need to pray a lot, keep close to the Lord, and stick to your guns about the things that, deep down, you are convinced need to change. At City Gates, the church's decision making process was highly democratic. Anything that happened, only happened if there was a consensus. Really big decisions had to wait until the church's annual general meeting before they could be ratified.

I, on the other hand, didn't believe in making decisions via drawn out meetings of committees, at all. I believed in anointed leadership and the governance of a group of elders who supported the main leader, and who were committed to a united vision. If a decision needed to be made, then it needed to be made quickly. After due prayer and consideration, of course, but without waiting for the AGM!

City Gates church used to meet on a Sunday morning, as most churches would, but then the Ghanaian congregation met on the Sunday afternoon. In my reconnaissance trips to the church, before becoming its minister, I had always attended a morning service, so really I'd never seen the "real" Ghanaian church in full flow. A number of things about it bothered me.

First there was the segregation. Men and women sat on opposite sides of the church. I had a big problem with that. But crucially, the meetings were conducted in *Twi* – the common Ghanaian dialect. This was fine for the Ghanaian community, but it presented a massive problem for any other visitors to the church. I knew it would be the most significant barrier to future growth. Of course, it was good and right for the Ghanaians to meet together for fellowship, but I believed that God wanted to create a church that represented the full spectrum of the cultural diversity that existed in the area.

There were other cultural "issues"…

When I arrived for my first Sunday afternoon meeting, I was confronted with what looked like a market in full swing. People were selling food and clothes on the street outside the church. It was probably what would have been happening if the church was located in Ghana, but this was Ilford, East London. I knew it had to change. How else could people from the local community, who'd grown up in Ilford, be able to access a church that was relevant to them?

Another aspect was the numerous dedications of children that took place. I think people must have come from all over London to have their children dedicated at the church, because never a Sunday went by when there wasn't a dedication. It wasn't a simple, brief ceremony either – people set up their video cameras and the dedications went on and on; they turned into massive productions. The result was that services were hijacked by the dedications week after week, and other important elements were squeezed out. This was something else that, as far as I could see, had to go. I made the decision that, from now on, we would only dedicate the children of church members.

The people of the church were incredibly patient with me as I changed many things that they had grown accustomed to, and I grew to love the people deeply. They had many outstanding qualities, the chief of which was their level of faith. They taught me so much about trusting God and expecting Him to do the miraculous. In many white, middle class, western churches I see a great desire for intimacy, but not always a great level of faith. Among black majority churches, faith is the predominant characteristic – faith that God can and will do much more than we can ask or imagine. They were also incredibly generous, with a strong emphasis on sowing and reaping, and they believed that if they gave sacrificially, they would never be in debt – something they proved to be true over and over.

Another characteristic of City Gates, as with all black majority churches, was the *honour* that was afforded to the senior minister. Honouring our leaders before God is a great thing, but taken to extremes becomes unhealthy. The reason the eldership sat on the platform during meetings was honour. But I was determined to demonstrate a model of servant leadership that included an appropriate, not excessive, level of honour. The esteem that was given to leaders was too much and needed to be tempered to a sensible level. I agreed that leaders should be respected, but not placed on a pedestal. I told the elders,

"Guys, I'm not sitting up there."

Of course, their response was, "But if you don't sit up there, we can't sit up there!"

"Exactly."

Nowadays, this has been embedded into our culture, so that some people call me pastor and others just "Steve", because they all feel comfortable around me, which is what I like. But to get there required a quantum shift in people's thinking.

How exactly did I go about changing this, you might wonder? I joined the church football team and played football with them every week. I got my hands dirty helping with very practical jobs that needed doing around the church. Once a couple of church members came into the building during the week and found me on my hands and knees fixing one of the urinals which was broken. They threw up their hands in horror: "Oh no, Pastor, you mustn't do that – let someone else fix it!" They did their best to drag me away from the task, but that was the point – I was just like anyone else in the church; it just so happened that the call of God on my life was to be their pastor. I constantly asked myself what Jesus would do, if He was in my position. I firmly believed that if the toilet was broken, Jesus would get on and fix it – and if that's what He was like, that's what I wanted to be like!

There is great security in being accessible as a leader. Today, my leadership team don't restrict me as their leader, yet there is great accountability between us. I would hate to be in that place where the leader is so revered that they are seen to be untouchable. With accountability comes safety. That's not to say I don't believe in strong leadership, because I do. Strong leaders create an atmosphere of security amongst their people. But there must be no room for them to abuse their position.

Changing the church culture from a slow-moving, committee-driven democracy, however, was more difficult. Glen, my associate, who had been used to a different style of leadership, really struggled with my leadership approach. In time, he would have taken on the leadership of another Elim church anyway, but perhaps this sped up his transition. As a leader, I had to be able to make certain decisions independently of the eldership, who all had full time jobs and family responsibilities to attend to. I'm not talking about major financial decisions but relatively simple decisions that any church leader has to take.

Remember, I had come from St Helens having been involved in a large building project that had culminated in us creating a spacious new church building in the town. I was used to carrying a certain level of responsibility and having to lead from the front. You can imagine my frustration, then, when I went out and bought an answering machine for the church, only to be told that I couldn't possibly introduce such a change without it first being discussed at a meeting and due democratic process followed!

Then there was the issue of the carpets. The existing ones were old, tired and worn out. They looked dreadful and I wanted to change them to smarten the place up. Of course, we needed to discuss this, at great length, in a committee meeting. Someone suggested cleaning them would be sufficient, but I was adamant – they had to go!

In a way, the answering machine and carpets came to my rescue, because I was able to sit down with the eldership team, citing them as examples of democracy gone mad and say, "I'm sorry guys, but this has got to change."

Then there was the worship…

Worship was conducted using just a piano and an organ. Both the musicians were, shall we say, "mature". During the first service I attended, they sang a hymn that was so old even I'd never heard of it.

Change is never popular – we know that – and there were people who were unhappy about all the changes I was making. So much so, that a very vocal section of the people began to speak out and question whether I really should be their minister. Things came to head at the AGM. I was trying to change the constitution to allow more freedom in leadership, so that the church could grow and progress, whereas others, not seeing the bigger picture just wanted to hold onto their democracy and the time-honoured way of doing things.

The turning point came when I addressed the whole church and said,

"Let me paint a scenario for you. If you insist on keeping your democracy, then you have the ultimate authority over me, your senior leader."

Everyone was horrified at the thought of this. Put like this, it was in direct conflict with their desire to honour, respect and trust me as their leader.

It was painful, hard work, and it took a long time, but I persisted in re-educating the church about biblical leadership – allowing leaders to lead, and to have autonomy within a framework of accountability. As we persisted, we began to see the church move from an inward looking, insular community, to an outward looking, multicultural house of God that could grow in significance.

13

TAKING UP THE CHALLENGE

———·———

Sometimes God will reveal the plans He has for our lives all in one go, so that we have a clear idea of where we are going and what it is we're are supposed to do. But in my experience, such "light bulb" moments are rare. More often than not, God takes us on a journey of unfolding revelation. We see ahead a bit at a time, not getting the full picture. As we move forward, trusting Him, however, He reveals more.

When our family arrived in Ilford, I didn't know specifically what it was that God had in mind for us to do there – other than to pastor the church in the way He wanted and reach out to the lost and broken around us. That was obvious, but what was the bigger picture?

In fact, when people asked me, "Steve, what is your vision for City Gates?" I would tell them honestly, "I don't have one!" This must have struck many people as odd, if not a little alarming, but the fact was that I trusted God to reveal the full vision for His work in the town in His time and His way.

Many new pastors, I'm sure, live under the pressure of producing a vision statement that sets out what they believe God is going to do with their church; plus the things that are on their own hearts to see happen. I didn't have one and I had no intention of producing one! How could I second guess what God was up to in East London? I didn't even know the place.

What I did know for certain was that God had called us and that was enough for me. We were definitely in the right place at the right time. The rest was up to the Lord. I was quite happy for Him to reveal His plans to us bit by bit.

Eventually, the Lord impressed on my heart that He would build a "large church in the heart of Ilford". Not just a numerically large one, but a *significant* one; a church that was large in *influence.*

On reflection, my "vision" for God's work has always been revealed through need. In other words, a clear need arises, I see it and begin to respond to that need, then, out of meeting the need God provides a clear vision of what He wants done and how. This was how City Gates' ministry to drug addicts in East London began.

One day I received a phone call from John Macy, who ran the UK base of the organisation Teen Challenge. I had previously been invited to get involved with the ministry and had accepted a place on their national board. Now John was asking if I would be willing to take a single decker outreach bus into the centre of Ilford. For those unfamiliar with it, Teen Challenge was founded in New York by David Wilkerson with the object of providing a "Christian faith-based solution to life-controlling problems, such as substance abuse…". It was a unique ministry that had proven effective in transforming the lives of countless addicts. I didn't have a single-decker bus just sitting around, but with John's request for help came the offer of provision.

"We'll give you a bus and also provide a member of staff for a year to help run the programme," he said.

Although I was an advocate and promoter of the great work of Teen Challenge, I was reluctant to take on this project. John's call came during the first year of our ministry in City Gates. It seemed too much to take on, considering all the other changes and challenges I was currently dealing with.

"No, John, I don't think I can take this on," I said. I was on the brink of ending the conversation and hanging up, but for some reason I just couldn't put the phone down. In the end I couldn't turn John down because I couldn't deny the reality of the need. I knew where I had come from. If I could help just one other person to find Jesus and find freedom from the vice of drug addiction, it had to be worth doing didn't it?

"OK, John," I eventually conceded. "I don't know how, but I'll do it."

The original intention had been for the project to be shared by a number of churches across the town. This would mean that it could be more easily resourced, with plenty of volunteers to go out on the bus and speak to addicts on the street. But when it came to the crunch, only one other church got involved besides City Gates.

We were to take the bus onto the Gascoigne Estate in Ilford – one the most deprived and notorious estates in London. Initially, I was worried that we wouldn't have enough people willing to get involved, but the church members stepped up, and as time went on more and more people from other churches got involved.

From the very beginning we saw people saved on the streets. Afterwards we would encourage them to join the Teen Challenge recovery programme, which meant travelling out to their rehabilitation centre in Wales. There they would be taken through the proven 6-step programme, which included:

1. *Recognition* of destructive and habitual thoughts that lead to substance abuse
2. *Focus* on healing the wounds of past failures and broken relationships
3. *Character* development and spiritual growth

4. *Continuing Care Planning* such as employment, education, housing, support systems and relapse prevention
5. *Re-entry* for those needing additional assistance in education, transitional housing, securing jobs etc.
6. *Restoration* to help those who had fallen back into old behaviour patterns

Of course, I soon realised that it wasn't always practical for people based in East London to travel to Wales to spend months in rehabilitation, and I wondered if there was a way that we could provide the same care/spiritual programme in our own town. But how? It must surely cost hundreds of thousands of pounds to employ a staff and create a properly functioning rehabilitation centre.

In the midst of all this, God miraculously opened a door, as only He can do, and it looked as though there might be a solution. One day a guy I'd never met before approached me and put forward an incredible proposal. He told me that he'd just sold his business to a multi-national corporation and made a lot of money. However, the large building he had been using was surplus to requirements to the corporation. They didn't want to pay rates on it, so they had suggested giving it to a charity to use. The man suggested that we could have use of the building for a "peppercorn" rent for five years. They were asking the ridiculous sum of £1 per year! It meant that, suddenly, we had a building available. If that was the case, then all we now needed was a suitable person to manage the establishment and operation of a new centre.

Around this time, unfortunately, I'd had some differences of opinion with the person Teen Challenge had appointed as our project coordinator. He was a great guy who, in my opinion, was functioning in the wrong role. The heart of our disagreement was that, fundamentally, he felt that what most addicts needed was deliverance. My view was that they needed love the most. In the end we had to agree to disagree and part company. This meant I needed to find someone else to run the operation that was beginning to take shape.

One day, I was driving home from a trip to Wales when Javier came to mind. Javier was a member of our church and had worked as a volunteer for Teen Challenge for a long time. I knew that he presently had a job working in a shoe shop in Walthamstow, but very clearly I felt God say to me that Javier was the man for the job.

I decided to act there and then and called Javier from my mobile. Instead of driving home, I diverted and began heading towards his house. On the phone I told him that I was coming round to see him and said what it was about – there was an opportunity for him to take on the project manager's job for Teen Challenge. I asked him to chat to his wife, Tracey, about it. I stopped short of saying, "God has told me you're the person for this job," which would have been manipulative. Instead I said, "I believe you'd be suitable for the role."

I arrived at Javier's and we talked things over. The salary we could pay for the job wasn't huge, but it was on a par with what he was already earning and, of course, he was perfectly suited to the task. But Javier had a problem – one which says a lot about the calibre of the man. He told me,

"When you first mentioned this to me, Steve, I thought, *I'd love to do this, but I can't.*"

"Why not?" I wondered.

"Well, over the past year the Lord has given me the opportunity to witness to lots of people in the shop. So I thought, if I leave, who's going to speak to them about Jesus?"

While he was waiting for me to arrive at his house, however, Javier had gone out for a walk to post a letter. On the way back he bumped into a friend of his, Byron – a Christian from another church – and they began to chat.

Javier didn't mention our conversation at all, but Byron said to him,

"I'm looking for a job. I don't suppose there are any jobs going at the shoe shop where you work?"

"Funny you should ask..." Javier replied.

Javier felt strongly that this was God confirming that he should, in fact, take on the project manager's role. God had honoured his commitment to preaching the gospel, sent him a replacement, and released him to take on the role.

We took possession of the building that was ours for just £1 per annum, named it Wilkerson House after the Teen Challenge founder, and began to renovate it to turn it into the first Teen Challenge rehab centre in East London.

In the beginning it functioned purely as a crisis centre. We were able to take in young lads in need for just three months, during which time we would help them as much as we could. As time went on, however, I became dissatisfied with this. The problem with only having someone for three months was that the staff never saw the results of their efforts – the boys were gone too quickly. I also questioned whether we were really serving them as individuals as well as we could in such a short space of time. So I began to put a case to the national board of Teen Challenge for us to become a full, residential centre. There was some resistance to this idea and our discussions became quite tense. I could really see the need to expand the scope of our ministry to those in need in our area, whilst the board was reluctant to see the focus shift away from their main rehabilitation centre in Wales. They were also concerned about taking on the liability of the new building we were renting, because my vision was to eventually buy it and make it our permanent base.

In the end, it was mutually agreed that Teen Challenge East London should be established as a new charity in its own right, and run by us in Ilford. We had in place the main resources that we needed, and the vision to take the ministry forward, so we were released to go and do it. It meant that we could work towards creating a year-long residential programme for the people who came to us for help.

We were granted significant funding for the project from the Government's Supporting People fund. Focused on housing provision, it would enable us to create the residential facilities we needed to take people in and care for them. But we quickly ran into trouble. The Head of Social Services in the area summoned Javier and me for a meeting and called into question what we were doing. He said outright that he wasn't happy with how we were set up and told us that we needed to become "less Christian".

I asked point blank, "Are you saying that if we don't, then you'll withdraw our funding?"

In so many words it was made clear that he would. We left the meeting and I said to Javier,

"If we take away the Christian aspect of what we're doing, then we might as well pack up and close the doors. I don't want to do it."

"Neither do I," he agreed. "It's not what we're about."

That day we made the decision to walk away from £300,000. But the Lord came to our rescue. One of the young men on the Teen Challenge programme was Matt Bott – a very clever guy who, before coming to us, had set up a business called Breakeryard. com. It enables people to source and buy car parts from breakers yards across the country at a big discount. Matt decided that he should plough some of the revenue from his business into Teen Challenge East London. It replaced the funding that we had lost.

Needless to say, all along the way there have been similar challenges, but God has proven Himself faithful time and time again. Through the ministry we have seen so many lives transformed that they alone could be the subject of another book.

14
THE SEARCH FOR A NEW HOME

Any pastor of a growing church will tell you that one of the greatest, most difficult challenges to contend with is that of space. Historically, many churches were planted in town centres in order to be located at the heart of their communities. But as a church grows and expands, it becomes more difficult to service its needs as it outgrows its surroundings. Multiple services is the answer many leaders come up with in response to this problem, but this stretches essential resources, sometimes too much. The more challenging answer is to get a bigger building! Not easy, given the price of prime location real estate.

As City Gates church grew, the need for more space became painfully obvious. In fact, I'd known from the beginning that this church, which existed in a one-room building, would soon have to face moving to a new home or somehow develop its existing site. The facilities we had were woefully inadequate. There were no additional rooms for ministries such as the children's work and the main room could seat about 250 people maximum.

During my time at St Helens I had learned a lot from David Tinnion about project managing the building of a new church centre and I knew that I would probably have to go through the same process. We would definitely need to do something – and soon.

Next door to our existing building was a modest sized piece of land that had come up for sale. Sandwiched between City Gates and the land was a bookshop that was run by a lady from a strict Brethren background, who was known not to be a fan of the Pentecostal church next door to her. Thinking forward, I could see that if we could acquire both the land and, one day, the site of the bookshop, then the overall space would have great potential for redevelopment.

I decided to raise the matter of purchasing the land at my very first eldership meeting – either a brave or foolhardy move. I suggested that it would be a good idea if we bought the land to give us some space for supporting ministries in the church, and with a view to future development. In short, the majority of the eldership were not up for this, except for one. Lector Williams, who would become one of my closest friends, agreed with me that we should be bold and go for it.

When I first visited City Gates, incognito, before accepting the leadership, Lector had been the person who introduced me to everyone. Lector is from the Caribbean and that day he wore a Hawaiian shirt, open almost to the waist, and sported a large medallion. He looked like an extra from a 1970's cop movie. But he was warm, generous, and a man of faith.

With Lector's support, the other elders were prepared to explore the idea of buying the land. We needed to raise £60,000 to purchase it and eventually decided to have an offering. The people gave generously and, over time, we were able to raise all the cash needed to buy the land. Once we took possession of it, as an interim arrangement we placed a couple of Portakabins there to house our children's work.

In time, another building near the church became available. It had been occupied by a group calling themselves the New Apostolic Church. One of their members knew one of ours and mentioned that they were about to put it on the market. Once again, we had discussions as an eldership and, with a raised faith level, eventually purchased it. We called it The Centre and it became our administrative base.

Next to the Centre was an old cinema which had closed down and one day that too came onto the market. It was up for sale for £1 million. To cut a long story short, we also made a bid to purchase that building. The day I announced to the congregation that we might make an offer for it there was an audible gasp. They couldn't believe that we might actually spend that amount of money. In the event, we didn't get the building, but looking back I can see that step by step, God was raising our faith levels in preparation for what He really wanted to do.

Before that, however, and as the church continued to grow, I continued to look for possible buildings for us to "grow into". One day Julia and I were driving past the old British Aerospace building on the edge of town and saw a For Sale sign. It was a large building and was on a terrific site with 3 acres of land. I made a note of the agent's phone number and, when I got back to the office, I called and asked how much the building was up for. The agent told me £8 million and I put down the phone without saying another word!

It seemed way beyond our capacity, just out of this world. Yet, the idea wouldn't leave me. It wasn't too far away from the town centre and it was on this huge site with so much scope. I spoke to my PA at the time, Vanessa, and asked her to write a letter to the agent saying that we would be prepared to pay £6 million for the building. It was an ambitious, some would say downright cheeky offer. But the building hadn't been in use for some time and, partly, I wanted to test how desperate they were to sell it.

I was very surprised then when the agent wrote back to say

that their client, BA, would accept an offer of £6 million. That was amazing. But now, of course, I had a problem. I hadn't mentioned the "offer" to anyone, so now I would have to tell everyone about it!

I recalled something that John Wimber once said – that the key to increasing people's vision had a lot to do with the right timing and location. In other words, you wouldn't raise people's level of faith or inspire them to think bigger by talking to them in the tiny back room of a church. They needed to "see" something greater to be able to grasp the bigger picture. As it happened, our leadership team were all going away together on a trip to South Korea. We were visiting Yoido Full Gospel Church and going to spend time on their Prayer Mountain. I decided to bide my time and talk about this possible building to everyone whilst in Korea.

Our first night in Seoul was spent at the church's missions house and we were surrounded by people who had come from all over the world. We were in an amazing place of prayer and faith and the atmosphere was electric. On that Friday night I told the guys that I had seen this building which we could purchase for £6 million. Unanimously they wanted to go for it. I'm sure that, in no small part, our location helped that decision.

When we returned to the UK we began the process of firming up our offer with the support of the Elim movement's headquarters. They would allow us to sell our present buildings in order to help fund the purchase. Over the next few months we had to spend a fair amount of money on obtaining permissions to use the site in the way we wanted, and we engaged the help of an expert planning consultant to help us do it. The first good news was that the vendor had accepted our offer. The second bit of good news was that the local council's regulatory committee voted unanimously for City Gates to acquire the building for a worship/community centre. We even won the support of the local press, and the local Imam and

Rabbi. Everything was going so well.

Then came a major bombshell. The economy, which had been in the doldrums, began to pick up and that meant property prices increased accordingly. Suddenly, a developer appeared on the scene and lodged a counter offer, putting far more money on the table than we could, to develop the land as a residential site. At this point in the proceedings, our offer which had already been accepted, was suddenly rejected in favour of this new offer.

This was a serious blow to our plans and, of course, we felt that it completely lacked integrity and should not have been happening. We discussed it as an eldership and decided that we weren't prepared to give up on the building that easily, so we asked for the matter to be put before an enquiry. The council had already granted us permission to use the site in the way we wanted and we understood that the new buyer was going for an alternative permission.

The resulting enquiry lasted a week. In the end the matter was escalated all the way to the desk of the Deputy Prime Minister at that time, John Prescott. In the end it was he who decided that the site should be used to create additional residential dwellings in the area. That meant we were effectively ruled out.

Our planning consultant, a wealthy man in his own right, was so incensed about the political machinations, and the vendor's change of mind, that there was some talk of the Government being taken to the High Court over this issue. Whether this was a serious prospect or not, unfortunately word of this rumour got out to the press and suddenly people realised that there could be a big battle over the site. As a result, the current owners immediately had the building demolished – thus scuppering our plans once and for all.

As you can imagine, all of this was upsetting, frustrating and disheartening. I personally felt the weight of responsibility for having spent church funds on getting to this point, only to have the rug pulled from beneath our feet. I couldn't understand what was going on.

It was at this point, as I was confronted with a flattened building that could have been our fantastic new church centre, that God spoke and said something that resonated deeply with me. It was this: *David was never anointed to be a giant killer, he was anointed to become king. Kingship was his primary function, not being a warrior.* As with David, the anointing of God will take you where you need to go in life, according to His purposes. I realised then that we didn't need to waste time fighting giants, but that God's anointing on us as a church would make a way for us. In the end, we would have what God wanted us to have, despite any obstacles that might stand in our way.

The old cliché says that God moves in mysterious ways. I prefer to say that God's provenance always goes before us. The statement issued by the enquiry said that the main reason for turning down City Gates in favour of the new developer was that the activities we wanted to carry out "should be done from the town centre, the heart of the community". Although it was a blow to us at the time, it was a blessing in disguise, because it set us up for the future.

Now our focus returned to our existing site and the bookshop sandwiched between us and our land. I wondered if perhaps it was time to try to acquire this building, giving us the whole site for a possible redevelopment. But there was the problem of the lady who owned it and her clear animosity towards the church. In the end, the way around this problem was for our planning consultant to create a new company in order to make the purchase. He approached the lady on our behalf. She was willing to sell in principle, but actually wanted a slightly different deal: a combination of some money and an appropriate place to relocate to. We agreed the sum of money and then began looking into how we might relocate her.

This is where things got slightly complicated, but it all worked out in the end! We heard that there was a church for sale called St Clements. We had also heard that the local NFI church, run by my friend, Robin Hawkins, were looking to sell their building and buy a new one. I alerted Robin to the availability of the St Clements' site and after looking at it, he decided it was perfect for them. Then we made an offer to buy his old NFI building! This was a three storey site. Once we had acquired the building, we offered the bookshop lady to relocate her shop to its ground floor.

The purchase of the bookshop went ahead and the lady relocated – still none the wiser that she had sold her building to the church next door. As things worked out, in time she decided that she wasn't particularly happy with her new location, so in the end we bought her lease off her and took control of the whole of the former NFI building, which in time we sold to developers.

This long and, seemingly circuitous, journey meant that we now had a complete site that we could redevelop. We began to develop plans to flatten the whole site and build, from scratch, an amazing new church centre. It would cost around £8.5 million to complete, but we would end up with a building far better than anything we'd looked at so far – and it would be where God clearly wanted us to be, right in the centre of the town.

Give a church to get a church

Of course, just as £1 million had seemed a stretch at the beginning, and £6 million for the BA building another astronomical sum, nearly £9 million was also "other worldly" in terms of our church finances. People were generous, but this was a big ask. God, however, spoke into the situation.

Prior to arriving in Ilford I had never travelled abroad to minister, only visiting churches across the UK. But around this time, Elim were looking for people to travel out to the Philippines. A group of churches there had become affiliated to the movement and they needed help in strengthening the church through solid Bible teaching. My area Superintendent, Gordon Hills, asked me if I would go, and I agreed.

Initially, I decided to go on my own. I met with the leaders of the churches there and gave some teaching and ministry. But even on that first visit, I knew God was up to something. He impressed upon me that this would not be a one-off visit, and that I should return and continue to build relationships. So, at the next opportunity, I returned there, this time taking others with me. Over time the relationship grew and in due course whole teams of people from City Gates would travel there.

City Gates is a multi-cultural church now, but at the time we hardly had any Filipinos in our congregation. Missions tended to arise out of a natural connection – people returning to their home nations to plant churches. If you were a Nigerian, you would go back and plant a church in Nigeria; or Ghana if you were Ghanaian, and so on. So it was unusual for us to be connected to the Philippines. At the same time I was pleased about this because it meant this was a *real* mission for people. There was no sense of self-interest, it was an act of sowing.

We kept going back to the Philippines simply because we felt it was a place we should continue to invest in. Then one day the Lord spoke to me from the verse in Luke 6:

"Give and it shall be given to you, pressed down and shaken together..." (v8)

Suddenly it hit me. God was saying that if we wanted His help in funding our church building, we should sow and give. I went to my eldership and shared what I believed God was saying. Put simply,

"I feel that God is saying if we want to *get* a building we've got to *give* one."

The churches based in Manila were growing, but there was a clear need for a good, well-equipped school to stand alongside them to serve the community. Everyone agreed that we should sow into this situation and help them to get the building they needed.

It may seem crazy to some people – to invest in someone else's building when you are trying to save up for your own, but such is the wisdom of God that so often appears to be upside down when considered only through the filter of human logic. So we set out to build a school in the Philippines. The people of City Gates supported this venture wholeheartedly and really grasped the principle of sowing into another situation, allowing God to bless us in ours.

We bought some land that had nothing much on it apart from one dilapidated building, flattened everything and then built a new structure. The main building was a school facility, then we later added out-buildings and a basketball court. The Academy, as it's called, is an amazing project which, at the time of writing, has just celebrated its tenth year. It stands like an oasis in the suburbs of Manila – an amazing school that takes in kids who are the poorest of the poor. There is also a thriving church on the site and it is changing people's lives. Kids are being well educated and having their life outlook transformed – and, of course, they are finding Jesus!

And, I believe that it is as a result of our obedience that God has provided for all our financial needs for our own building.

15
FATIGUED BUT STILL IN PURSUIT

Before I became seriously addicted to drugs I had always been very sporty. I was a very useful footballer, and I played rugby league and excelled at that too. I eventually went on to play fullback for St Helens and we toured Europe, as well as the UK, winning a number trophies.

Having abused my body for so many years though – asking more of it than anyone has the right to and still survive – I decided to get serious about my health again and see if I could actually prolong my life by getting properly fit. As many pastors will tell you, often ministry life is not conducive to a healthy life. It doesn't have to be that way, but the fact is, pastors are so incredibly busy, juggling many different concerns, that personal health and fitness can slip further and further down the list of priorities.

Leading a sedentary lifestyle meant that I had piled on the weight and at one point I weighed around 16 Stone, and I'm not exceptionally tall. It wasn't until one day when I happened to see myself on video and thought, "Oh no! Look at the size of me!" that I knew I needed to do something about it. I felt really unfit and I didn't like it.

In our church was a lady called Beverley Escoffrey, who was a professional personal trainer. She was already working with a couple of guys from the church, so I joined them. Every Monday Bev put us through our paces in Barking park. By the end of these sessions I was absolutely finished. After several such workouts I wasn't sure I could cope with the boot camp style approach any more, so I began running.

I started jogging and, like most people who suddenly begin running for the first time, was well out of breath before I'd reached the end of my road. But I persisted and went out for a run every night. Day by day, I slowly got a bit better at it, and ran a bit further. Little by little I improved and before long I'd got the bug for it. I began to go on regular runs, gradually building up the distance, and thoroughly enjoying it.

Runners will tell you that there is nothing quite like a run to clear the mind of the debris we accumulate during the course of a day. Although your body is engaged in hard work, your mind clears, and you can also engage with God in a meaningful way as all distractions are put to one side.

Not long into my new regime I saw an advert for the London Marathon. A crazy idea came into my head. *What if I ran a marathon?* Really? An entire marathon? It seemed ambitious – because it was! But I'd heard that it was actually quite hard to get accepted, so I thought I had nothing to lose by applying; I probably wouldn't get in anyway. I applied and was promptly accepted via their ballot scheme.

I was still carrying a fair amount of weight at the time and, frankly, I wasn't running that far, so people probably thought I had lost my mind. But the marathon was six months away and so I decided to dedicate that time to training for it. I went all out for it and lost masses of weight.

The day of the marathon came and I successfully managed to get round and complete the run – though not without causing Julia some concern. When I got to the end she took one look at me and said, "Steve! You look green!" My abiding memory of that day is the agony I was in at the end – not while I was running, but trying to walk down the stairs to the Underground afterwards!

* * *

Fast forward several years and I had just completed my seventh London Marathon. I was thrilled to have been able to complete another successful run. It went well and I was on a high afterwards, feeling fantastic. It was then that I was hit with a real curve ball.

One afternoon I was walking through Ilford town centre, returning to the church office after lunch, when I saw a mobile NHS unit parked up, its staff handing out literature to the public. One of them stepped forward and gave me an information card. It was all about the Hepatitis C virus. I glanced over it. It said that some 200,000 people in the UK were walking around with the Hep C virus and they didn't even know it. I registered this fact, but then thought little more about it.

A couple of nights later I sat down to watch the evening current affairs programme *London Tonight* and an item came on about Hep C. A number of high profile celebrities suffered with it – Pamela Anderson, Steven Tyler of Aerosmith, Anita Roddick of The Body Shop amongst them. They also interviewed a local guy who had it and I was struck by the fact that his background was very similar to mind.

"That's just like me," I thought. "He's done pretty much everything I've done in life."

These two events seemed a bit more than coincidence to me and I ended up going to see my doctor for a health check, which included a routine blood test. Some time later, when the results came back, the doctor asked to see me because the blood test had shown up "an abnormality".

"Mr Derbyshire," my doctor told me, "I really must encourage you to stop drinking so heavily."

My blood test had shown up a problem with my liver function. The doctor assumed it was because I was a heavy drinker.

"I don't drink," I replied, surprised. The truth be told I wasn't a big fan of alcohol anymore and didn't really like it. Straight away I felt I knew what the real issue was.

"I know what it is, doctor," I told him, "it's Hepatitis C."

We talked further and the doctor agreed that we needed to do a second blood test to confirm whether this was indeed the case. It came as no surprise when the results came back positive. I had genotype 2 Hep C. Type 2 is not as serious as type 1, and is a little more easily treated, but the fact is, it's still hard to get rid of. The doctor also told me that between my first and second blood tests, the viral load had substantially increased (the volume of viral particles that are circulating through the blood).

I was dismayed by this news. This virus had been lying dormant in me for 30 years and now it had started to come alive – now, when I'd never been fitter or felt better! It was ironic.

Of course, I must acknowledge the fact that I had lived a lifestyle that made me totally vulnerable to the disease. I had shared needles with other addicts, and used dirty needles over and over again. You name it, I had done it. Now all of that was catching up with me and the virus was attacking my liver.

I talked it over with Julia, feeling very sorry for myself as I plunged into something of a crisis of faith. I had been supernaturally saved from drugs, but now this had come back to bite me.

"I thought I'd been set free of this," I told her.

Julia was straight with me – and I'm so glad she was. It's amazing how a great partner can rescue you from negative thinking.

"Well, you haven't been, you've got it," she told me. "But you can thank God that He set you free from the addiction. You've just got to trust Him and cope with this as best you can."

She was absolutely right. I just had to trust God to get me through this crisis – whatever that might involve – just as He had already brought me through so many things on my journey.

I began treatment for the condition – interferon and ribavirin – and soon realised that it was going to be a long, hard road to recovery. The effects of the drugs used to treat Hep C are heavy duty – almost as bad as chemotherapy. I had to inject myself in the stomach once a week and this would have to continue for six months. I didn't want to tell the church what I was going through, so I kept quiet about it and got on with the treatment, going about my usual daily duties.

Although the treatment only lasted 6 months, the effects of the treatment continued for a whole 12 months. Prior to treatment I had felt absolutely fantastic. Now, in order to get better, I felt really dreadful. The effects were twofold: both physical and mental/emotional.

After a day at the church office I was completely exhausted, I literally had nothing left. I discovered that there is a big difference between being *really tired* and *fatigued*. I was suffering from a deep fatigue that meant when I slumped into my armchair at the end of the day, I was certain I'd *never* get out of it again. I was physically and mentally spent.

More disturbing than the fatigue, however, were the mental and emotional effects. Unexpectedly, I became extremely introverted and disappeared into myself for very long periods. Coupled with this was an odd numbing of the emotions. I'd never experienced anything like it before, not even during the depths of drug addiction and, thankfully, have never experienced its like since. I simply *stopped feeling* and disappeared into a kind of grey ambivalence. I didn't love anything (or anyone), didn't hate anything, and there was nothing in between.

This twilight world was a dangerous place to live, especially for a pastor. It was pointed out to me, and I subsequently realised, that in this state of ambivalence one can say things that can be very upsetting and distressing to others. The worse thing is, you don't even realise you're saying them. During this time, I never missed a single Sunday of church – I was always there, come what may. The congregation were very gracious to me, but people must have wondered, what on earth is wrong with Pastor Steve, he's not himself – and I wasn't.

Once I understood the full impact of the effects, I had the foresight to warn my immediate staff that I would be a bit different for a few months, and that if I said anything that anyone found offensive, I didn't intend it; it wasn't personal! For my part, I endeavoured to be very considered and careful about how I communicated with people, thinking hard about what I was going to say before I said it.

Of course, the person who suffered the most during this time was Julia. She had to cope with a constantly exhausted husband and also caught the worst of my current lack of empathy for others. I threw all my effort into carrying on as normal, as far as my pastoral duties were concerned, which meant that it was outside of church hours where I tried to recuperate. Julia said that she basically "lost" me for a year. It was a tough time for us both, but Julia was great about it. She was very sensitive and just let me get on with handling it my way. She never complained or said too much about it. She was just there for me. Later, when it was all over, she simply said to me, "I've missed you."

At one point I felt I had to announce to the church what was going on, because it was obvious. The City Gates people were amazing as ever. I told them that I didn't want to be made a fuss of, and that I couldn't handle too much sympathy. I didn't want people to go over the top. Neither did I want people constantly quoting Bible verses at me. "I am actually spending time with God," I told them! (Sometimes I think the church can be one of the worst places to be sick, as well as one of the best ones, because people get funny ideas about sickness and spirituality or come out with unhelpful platitudes).

This whole experience was a real wilderness time for me. The spiritual wilderness is that place where deep testing takes place and the real priorities of life come into sharp focus. Everything that is inconsequential quickly fades away. But near the beginning someone gave me a word from the Lord from Scripture. This was no platitude. Judges 8 recounts an episode from the life of Gideon, where he is chasing hard after a goal – to defeat the enemy of God's people. Verse 4 says,

"They were exhausted, but still in pursuit."

Matthew Henry's commentary on this verse says, "Gideon's men were fatigued … yet eager to do more against their enemies." He goes on to say that this can often be the case; that in the Christian life we will find ourselves "fainting and yet pursuing".

This verse was pivotal for me. I realised that though I was deeply fatigued, I was still in pursuit – of God, of His purposes for my life, for City Gates, for the community of Ilford. God had not changed, despite my current adverse circumstances.

It was 2012 when I had the blood test that came back negative, meaning I'd received the "all clear". I was through the worst – though I still felt terribly sick and this would last for several months longer. Unfortunately, interferon is not like aspirin – it has a slow building, cumulative effect and takes a long time to leave your system.

Looking back, I reflect on the fact that God ultimately brought good to me out of this wilderness time. It made me a better person, a better pastor. It helped me understand sickness more; it gave me more compassion and empathy for others. God spoke to me many times during this period. His presence was constant, unwavering. He showed me that I could still be in pursuit of His presence, His purposes, even though I was limited by illness – and this was just as true for others as it was for me. He taught me a lot about the importance and value of relationships – that at the end of the day, Christianity is all about loving God and loving others. That is the heart of our faith.

Coming out of the wilderness, I was ready for action, and more determined than ever to pursue all that God wanted to do through City Gates. At the time of writing, I've also completed 19 marathons in many different cities of the world!

16
THE MIRACULOUS ESCAPE

The plans for our site redevelopment began to come together. Initially we thought of creating a multi-purpose building – something that would have many different uses for the local community – but God spoke to us very clearly about it being a *centre for worship*. Then we thought about possibly creating a suite of apartments on the very top of the building, which we could let out and use to create an income stream to fund the building, but again God spoke to us saying we weren't to put anything else on top of the building because we were to "seal it for future generations". We altered our plans accordingly and began to pursue the building project.

Building in a town centre is far from easy. There is a multiplicity of issues to consider and negotiate with the powers that be. Whatever you want to create has to fit in with everything else around it and all kinds of factors come into play. Without going into all the ins and outs, we had, for instance, to pay for an assessment of how our structure would affect the quality of light for those around it – where its shadow would be cast at midday etc. We had to pay for an environmental expert to assess the "green" impact of the cars that would occupy our parking spaces – and so on.

But we were granted outline planning permission and the build began officially in June 2011. The present buildings were demolished and work on the new building began. The new floor went in and the steel work went up. The new building would be a five-floor construction, though the building itself would be higher than five floors, because each floor was taller than normal.

As a church, we had already begun to meet weekly at Cineworld, at the end of the same street. We had far outgrown our existing building, which we only used for midweek activities. Now, each week as we met at the cinema, our members could walk past the building site and see progress being made, little by little. It was a hugely exciting time. The church looked forward to our new building with a huge sense of anticipation. We had a team of people who faithfully set up and packed away all the equipment we needed each week at Cineworld, who were looking forward to having a permanent place more than most! But all of us looked forward to leaving our nomadic existence behind and settling into our new home.

When the final floor at the top of the building was installed, someone suggested we have a "topping off" ceremony – a normal event for a major build like this, as the last bit of steel work goes in. We did this and took lots of photos and some video. It was attended by the mayor and other dignitaries and Steve Thompson, our worship leader, led us in worship as we sang *Jesus, Be the Centre*. It was an incredible moment. We showed the topping off service to the church that Sunday, which was greeted with rejoicing.

A couple of days later, on the following Tuesday, I was attending a Willow Creek conference in Bracknell with my staff, listening to Andy Stanley speaking about vision. It was a day I'll never forget – the last day of January, 2012. Part way through the day, Steve Thompson received a phone call. He came and tapped me on the shoulder; he looked shocked and agitated.

"Steve," he said, "your building is collapsing!"

I thought it was some kind of weird, bad taste joke.

"What? No!"

"Steve, it's true," he said.

I couldn't believe what I was hearing. I went outside. My face obviously told a story, because Julia and my staff gathered around me, looking concerned. I told the others what Steve had said and there was shock and tears all round. My next thought was to call our architects, Jeremy Emmerson and Steve Luxford.

"I'm hearing that the building has fallen down," I stated, feeling numb.

"I'm sorry, it's true Steve," Jeremy told me. "Most of it has collapsed, but there is still debris coming down."

I couldn't get hold of the construction company's site manager, Julian. More than anything I wanted to know: *had anyone been killed?* If so, this was a worse disaster than anything I could imagine.

I gathered my team together and said, "OK, let's get in the car. We need to get back to Ilford."

I tried calling Julian again but couldn't get through. Meanwhile, a member of my staff, Grace, was searching for news reports on the Internet in the back of the car. News of the disaster had indeed broken and, to our horror, initial reports were vague about whether or not there were fatalities. They seemed to suggest that there had been. My mobile phone was ringing constantly as people from all over the place – even Dubai and the US – called to see if what they were hearing was true and if I was OK. All I could do was respond, "I don't know, I've only just heard myself."

News was still pouring out via different media channels, but the information was confused and contradictory. One report said that a helicopter with heat-seeking equipment was hovering over the site looking for bodies. Eventually, I was able to raise Julian on the phone and asked him straight:

"Julian, has anyone been killed?"

Relief and thankfulness to God washed over me as he confirmed,

"No one has been killed, Steve."

If anyone had died on our site, I don't know how we could have carried on. I had to ask twice and Julian promised me that everyone was fine. He said he would tell me exactly what had happened in due course.

* * *

I visited the site the next morning. Words cannot adequately describe the feeling of seeing the scene of utter devastation that lay before me, a tangle of twisted steel and shattered concrete. I was heartbroken. Then I found out about the miracle which had saved the lives of around 20 men.

On the day of the collapse a large team of bricklayers had been on site. At 3.30pm, quite unexpectedly, the daylight deserted them and it became too dim to carry on working. The decision was made to leave the site for the day. Many other people, who were walking through the town centre that day, later reported that it suddenly became "dark" and "eerily quiet". The builders began to exit the site from 3.30pm onwards. At 4.15pm the building collapsed. No one got hurt.

Next door to our site is a council building. Our falling building scraped down the side of their building. The people who work there said that they felt the building shake and heard the rumble and shriek of twisting steel as it came down. The falling rubble wrote off seven cars which were sitting in the car park. Everyone agreed that it was a miracle no one was even injured, let alone killed. People later commented that there were people who might have been caught in the path of falling debris, who that day had left the office early for a variety of reasons. Many similar stories emerged later – too many to be a coincidence. The Lord in His mercy had saved many lives.

In the middle of the building, the huge crane, which only had a few feet of space around it, had somehow stayed erect whilst everything else had fallen away. If the crane had come down too, it would certainly have caused so much more damage and undoubtedly loss of life.

* * *

When we'd arrived back in Ilford on the previous evening it had seemed abnormally dark. Of course, there was chaos in the town centre. Our building was on the corner of two busy thoroughfares and was a main bus route. Grace found out that our people had organised a town wide prayer meeting and they wanted me to be there. I was upset, in shock and, initially, I didn't want to go to it, but Grace insisted.

"You've got to go, people need to know that you're OK."

Later, as I arrived at the meeting, I was ambushed outside by the press – local media, but also journalists from the *Telegraph* and *Guardian*. At first I wanted to avoid them like the plague, but then I felt God prompt me to speak to them. I told them that the events of this day were only half the story that would be told in coming years. I asked them to promise that, in due course, they would tell the *full* story:

"One day that building will be completed, and I want you all there when we open its doors."

Inside, the prayer meeting was absolutely packed with people – all of them praising God loudly and giving thanks, despite our present circumstances. To me, this said everything anyone ever needed to know about the quality of the City Gates church family and their incredible faith.

* * *

The collapse of the building was caused by a fabrication problem. It was being held together with a 35-tonne truss which had failed, meaning that the building had collapsed from top to bottom, not bottom to top as is usually the case. It was highly unusual because one fault shouldn't bring down an entire building. But it proved that, in fact, the building wasn't robust enough. It wasn't the fault of our construction company, but no more can be written about the issue at this time as the details are part of on-going legal proceedings.

In the past, when we had tried and failed to secure the British Aerospace building, spending quite a lot of money in the process, I'd had to stand in front of the whole church and tell them what had happened. It wasn't a nice moment, to put it mildly. That had been difficult, but what now? I wondered what I could possibly say to the people this time. At the next service, however, I was greeted with nothing but grace and support. People crowded around and laid hands on me. It's hard put into words how this spurred me on to see things through. I don't think some church members appreciate how their support and encouragement can boost their leader to fulfil God's vision – or how withdrawing their support or being discouraging can undermine their faith and confidence. Thankfully, the people of City Gates responded brilliantly and I never once heard anyone complain. Not even the set-up and pack-down teams! Everyone just rolled up their sleeves and got on with the job.

It was time to regroup, gather our courage, and look to the future again, dependent on God. We believed that He would work out His purposes. Our job was simply to cooperate, follow His lead, and persevere.

The day after

It wasn't until the next day after the collapse that I was able to properly visit the site and speak to the construction team about what had happened. But first I had to go into the church office and speak to the staff. This was the least difficult of all the conversations I would have about the disaster; they were so supportive.

Often, when visiting speakers came to City Gates, they would remark on the quality of our people. "You may not be the biggest church," someone once said, "but the depth of spirituality of your people is something really special and unique." This is so true. I really had no words for my staff, but I could see that they were OK and together we would face whatever came next.

I did, however, approach the site of our wrecked building with an awful sense of dread. I went there with my friends, Chris Thompson, Steve and Velveta Thompson, and Steve and Anouscha McEwen. We sat in a café next door and talked for a while before I went onto site. They had come to give me moral support – at that point, the site was cordoned off and I was the only person allowed to go near it. I was also blessed by the support of so many others who left messages or sent texts – friends, but also the leaders of many other churches.

I rarely listened to Premier Radio, being more of a news than music person when it comes to the radio, but for some reason I did that morning and was amazed to hear someone talking about me. In fact, he was talking directly *to* me. To this day, I'm not sure who the man was, but he had obviously heard the news reports and said,

"I just want to say to Steve Derbyshire: you keep fighting! I've seen you over the years and you're a warrior. Keep fighting the good fight of faith."

It's hard to describe what an incredible encouragement it was to hear these words. Our God is a good God!

As I went onto the site, there were twenty-five or so people there – the majority of them bricklayers who had been working on the site the previous day – walking around in shock. Many of them had simply turned up for work that morning, because they hadn't even realised what had happened. They were as shocked as anyone at the sudden devastation.

I asked if I could speak to all the workers, together, as a group.

"Most of you could have died last night," I told them. "You can see what's happened; you know that. If you hadn't clocked off early, you would all have been on site when the building came down. But as a church we pray for you, and everyone on site, every week, and I believe that God intervened to prevent a tragedy. You don't deserve His grace, just as I don't, but God loves each one of us. God's love protected you last night."

As I spoke, tears ran down the cheeks of some of these "tough" builders; even "Big Stan" a 6ft 5", 20 stone hulk of a guy who, on one occasion I'd somehow managed to prevent from punching his boss when a heated disagreement broke out between them. Finally, I told them,

"After today you guys will probably never work here again, and I'll probably never see you again. But please remember this one thing: we will still be praying for you; God loves you, and Jesus Christ died for you."

Meanwhile, the site was the scene of utter chaos. The Health & Safety Executive were crawling all over the site, interviewing everyone, and all the construction workers were fearful of prosecution. *Whose fault was this?* they were thinking. *Who's to blame?* It would take an awfully long time to get to the bottom of what had happened, and why.

The area around the wreckage-strewn site was still eerily quiet and the impact of the accident was far reaching. Opposite our building is a multi-storey car park. 200 cars were stuck there, unable to leave. All the businesses around had had to close temporarily. Similarly, workers were not allowed to go to work in the council offices next door. The buses that rumbled past the building at regular intervals had been diverted. I left the site wondering, "What next, Lord?"

The next day I met with our architect. In the aftermath of such a disaster it's amazing how quickly relationships change. Suddenly everyone is being very careful about what they say – not much, preferably nothing if possible – because of the legal implications. Their professional liability insurers would have told them to say nothing, whilst the lawyers began to get involved.

The long and short of that meeting was this:

"Steve, this is going to take a long time to sort out."

This was an apt summary. From that day, work would not recommence on the site for another three years. We entered into long-haul legal proceedings that would take all of that time to resolve, and more. In part, things are still being resolved. It has cost a great deal of time, money, and considerable amounts of prayer. But God is faithful and we can testify to His miraculous intervention and help.

* * *

Our building collapsed on 31 January, 2012. This chapter is being written on 31 January, 2016 – four years to the day. At the time of writing, our new building is two months away from completion and we are heading towards a very special day, where the church will take possession of its new home and we can look forward to what God will do in and through this new centre of worship.

The last four years have been a hugely stretching experience for me personally. I've dealt with things that I never imagined

I'd have to deal with as a minister. It has cost me more than a few sleepless nights. But adversity grows us as individuals. Going through and emerging from tough times makes us bigger people. What has been important for me has been to always keep hold of the bigger picture. I would say to other leaders who are going through challenging times: keep your courage and, whatever the details of your current difficulties, don't lost sight of the bigger picture of what God has called you to do. In the end, this is what will help and sustain you.

During all our challenges, the faithfulness of God has been a constant. Despite the roller coaster journey we've been on, He has never wavered or changed one bit. Though we may struggle to understand some of the things that have happened, He has never relinquished control of the situation. Perhaps the greatest miracle of all is that, through all of this, City Gates will be entering this incredible new facility, which has cost nearly £9 million to build, debt free. *To God be the glory!*

17
EPILOGUE: OUT OF THE RUINS

—·—

Thank you for reading this book. Above all, I hope the message that comes across loud and clear is that *God will lead you if you trust in Him*. In an earlier chapter, I mentioned the fact that I didn't have a clear vision mapped out when I arrived at City Gates. I was prepared to trust Jesus, day by day, and I knew that He would provide a vision for what He wanted me to do, which would come in response to particular needs. It's great to have a vision and a strategy, but it's much more exciting to be led on an adventure by the Holy Spirit. As we follow Him, gradually, God opens our eyes to what can be in our life, in our situation.

This book will be published on the day that City Gates church enters its new building. From the beginning, as we embarked on this ambitious project, God spoke to us about His purposes for the church in Ilford, and unfolded further revelation as we followed Him, step by step. After the collapse of the first structure, when it seemed as though all our dreams lay in ruins, God was still speaking. He had not changed His mind. It was clear that to Him, at least, that this disaster was no obstacle to accomplishing His will!

In the early days of seeking a permanent, suitable home for the church, a group of us prayed regularly and laid hands on the walls of our existing building. During that time God gave us many clear prophetic words and said "big" things that, on the surface, seemed impossible – unattainable without supernatural intervention. One such word was a promise from Isaiah 2:2:

"In the last days, the mountain of the Lord's *house will be the highest of all – the most important place on earth. It will be raised above the other hills, and people from all over the world will stream there to worship."* (NLT)

Ilford is home to a diverse mix of faiths. God has planted City Gates right in the middle of the town, with a building that is "raised above" those around it. It is one of the most prominent features of the landscape. I believe God has put us here for a reason – that His intention was to light a beacon in this place; to create a centre of worship that people will stream into.

Building local churches is so vital. Looking back, everything that I am, and all that I have, came as a result of being planted in a local church: my salvation, my wife and family, my ministry, the teaching I received, my opportunities for ministry... all came through the church. I love the local church and I'm committing the rest of my life to continuing to build it.

* * *

When I first began taking drugs, I honestly believed that I knew exactly what I was doing. I was in control and thought drugs would never have a hold on me; I could stop anytime I wanted to...

I was so utterly wrong. It wasn't until I tried to give up drugs that I realised I was completely addicted and couldn't stop. Hopelessness engulfed me. I saw no future ahead, just the downward spiral of an addict's life.

Deep inside, where no one else could see, I was searching for the real reason for my existence. I had no purpose for living – in which case I might as well be dead. I was empty. Taking drugs was just an attempt at escaping the awful reality of my life.

Jesus, however, took hold of me and radically changed my life. As well as supernaturally delivering me from the grip of hard drugs,

He gave me a hope and a future.

He can do the same for you.

You may not have a problem with drugs, though you may struggle with an addiction to something else – sex, gambling, any number of other things. Even if you don't have an addiction problem, you may recognise the fact that you are struggling in life. It could be due to the pain of past abuse, broken relationships, or knowing that you are just not living the life you know you were born for.

The problem is never the *real* problem. The problem I had – that we all have – was the spiritual vacuum inside that needed to be filled. This can only be filled by one thing: *the presence of God.* Drink, drugs, sex, power or achievement can never fill that void, only Jesus.

Jesus is the truth and only He can set you free. As my dad once said to me, "Give Him a chance, and He'll prove Himself true to you." As a person searching for meaning, my first proper prayer was as unsophisticated as they come:

"God, if you're there, help me!"

All God is looking for is sincerity, so He answers prayers like that. If you've never prayed this prayer before in your life, pray it now. Seek out a local church and get to know some Christians. Above all, remember that whatever you have done in your life until now, however messy you feel your past is, God can restore you. He is the Master of bringing hope out of the ruins.

———•———

For more information, visit us at:

http://www.citygates.london